Heart healthy cookbook for Beginners

Delicious quick and easy low-sodium and low-fat recipes to stress-free your heart and live a healthy life/30-day eating plan.

By

Allison Carter

EXTRA BONUS

Go to the last pages and frame the QR codes and access these great bonus gifts for you

Table of Contents

Introduction

Your heart health is an essential aspect of your life. In fact, having a solid and healthy heart is the starting point of health and well-being in general.

In this book, we will see in detail how to take care of your heart and, in general, the whole body and try to have a healthy, balanced, and above all, cheerful lifestyle.

Often, a person starts a diet or eating regimen trying to lose weight and lose weight. However, it is not clear why, but after a certain period, this person (in more than 92% of cases) returns to the original weight and still feels frustrated.

With the simple and clear indications in this book, you will find the best shape for you and understand the basic mechanisms to take care of the health of your heart in an incisive way.

We will therefore see that it is not necessary to radically change one's life but rather to assume and adopt "healthy" and "positive" behaviors for your health in general and specifically for your heart.

We will then see what the main risk factors that can trigger your heart health in the short and long term are; we will also know which the main foods are indicated, and which are better to avoid (or in any case, eat in small doses and above all rarely) to have a strong and healthy heart. We will see later the basis and the principle of operation for the diet that will take care of your heart forever.

By applying these simple behaviors, you will know your heart and bodywork in depth. Subsequently, seeking health with your diet, movement, and human relationships will be spontaneous and natural.

At the end of this book's introductory part, we will also look at what the America Heart Association says. Visiting their site daily makes it possible to take a cue from simple behaviors to adopt when certain disorders or discomforts related to our hearts occur.

Unique recipes have therefore been included to restore your metabolism and thoroughly purify your body while maintaining the robust health of your heart and all the connected organs.

At the end of this cookbook, you will finally find a 30-day meal plan indicating to have no thought about choosing the best food to start with. In fact, following the menu, you won't have to count calories or the value of fats, carbohydrates, and proteins to have balanced and correct foods from a purely nutritional point of view.

Every single recipe has therefore been designed for you so as not to weigh you down and to respect the general health of your heart and your entire metabolism.

Nutrition is an essential aspect to consider, and often many people overlook this fact. Diet and food will therefore be your next starting point to start taking care of your heart correctly; however, diet alone is not enough; it is also necessary to combine it with a correct, positive, and healthy lifestyle.

But now, let's start taking care of our hearts, and let's go!

CHAPTER 1: What are the risk factors for heart disease?

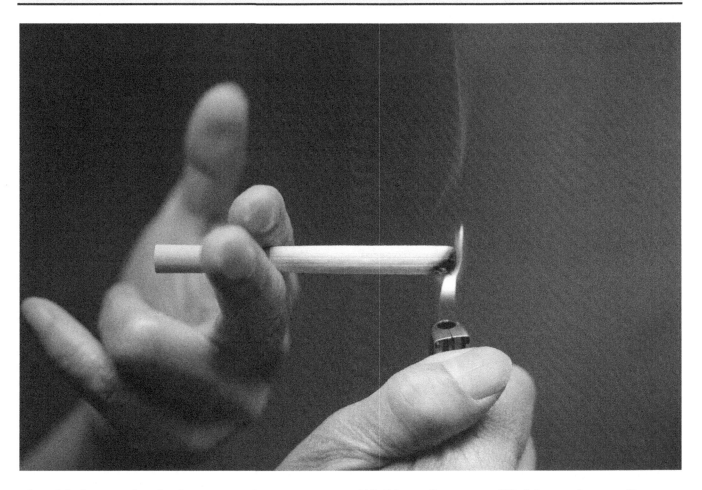

The risk factors for the heart are of two types: modifiable and non-modifiable. Both contribute to the possible onset of diseases such as heart attacks and strokes. However, non-modifiable risk factors are those on which you cannot act directly but whose effect can be mitigated thanks to good behavior and prevention measures.

AGE

The risk of developing cardiovascular disease is undoubtedly related to age. For example, myocardial infarction is more frequent in subjects between 50 and 60. SEX At young and old age, heart attack and atherosclerosis are more common in men than women. With menopause, on the other hand, the risk between men and women is equal.

FAMILIARITY

In the current state of scientific knowledge, the predisposition to cardiovascular diseases cannot be attributed to a single genetic factor but rather to a plurality of genes.For this reason, establishing the burden of familiarity with heart disorders is not easy.

The Interheart study published in The Lancet has estimated that, in which one of the two parents has had a cardiovascular event, this risk factor represents only one percent of the overall risk of falling ill. A minimal value, therefore. More recent studies have come to different conclusions. According to experts, if in a family there are close relatives who suffer or have suffered from heart disease, the risk seems to increase significantly: it seems to double for the siblings due to shared lifestyles and a common genetic predisposition. Coronary artery disease is defined in these cases as a "family unifying element" because it is found with a much higher frequency than hitherto thought. This happens if a heart attack or stroke occurs at a young age; the risk seems to increase in the more affected subjects within the same family. However, it should be noted that familiarity is often presented incorrectly, creating unjustified apprehensions. Family history of coronary artery disease exists in children of parents who had a cardiac event (heart attack or angina) before the age of 55 (in the case of the father) or before the age of 65 (in the case of the mother). Still, it is not always possible to trace parents' medical history. Suppose it is possible to rule out coronary artery disease in the parents with certainty. In that case, a familial predisposition in the children can be ruled out. If, on the other hand, there is the certainty of cardiac events in the parents, the probability of having a family predisposition is around 40-60 percent. However, it is good to remember that even if familiarity increases cardiovascular risk regardless of other risk factors, it does not necessarily imply that children will get heart disease. Rather than condemnation, family events should instead be experienced as a warning to take prevention from a young age.

MENOPAUSE

The cardiovascular risk for women and men is different, and gender represents a real risk factor. Men are naturally subject to higher blood pressure and heart rate and are more exposed to cardiovascular disease. In women, the risk changes at different stages of life: in childbearing age, the hormone estrogen, produced by the body regularly during the menstrual cycle, has a protective effect on the heart and blood vessels. During menopause, estrogen production ceases, and the danger of being affected by a cardiovascular disease increases significantly. The differences concerning the male gender are reduced to zero. The lower incidence of cardiovascular disease in women (until menopause) generates a paradoxical situation: women are at a disadvantage both in terms of the control of modifiable risk factors because they are less aware of the problem and in the case of accidental disease, which can be diagnosed with more significant delay. Furthermore, epidemiological studies on cardiovascular disease in women were started considerably later, and our scientific knowledge is more limited. Women over the age of 60, in the period of greatest cardiovascular vulnerability, make up a considerable proportion of patients in the general population, which is why it is necessary to promote a culture of female cardiological prevention to raise awareness among women on the subject.

THE CARDIOVASCULAR RISK CHARTER

many scientists and doctors have drawn up the cardiovascular risk map, a series of tables that make it possible to calculate the individual risk of suffering a major cardiovascular event (heart attack and stroke), fatal or non-fatal, in the next 10 years, for people between 40 and 70 who have not already undergone one. This card is a valuable tool available to general practitioners, but it is also available online. The form must be filled in with personal data such as age, gender, blood sugar, total cholesterol and HDL (a recent blood sample is required), and maximum blood pressure. It is also necessary to specify if you are on antihypertensive therapy if you are diabetic and a smoker. Through these simple data, the program will show the extent of your cardiovascular risk over the next ten years with three different possible outcomes: mild, moderate, or severe. On the other hand, modifiable risk factors are those factors that the environment and lifestyle can directly influence, both positively and negatively. Or:

- Arterial hypertension
- Hypercholesterolemia
- Diabetes
- Smoke
- Obesity/sedentary lifestyle
- Excess alcohol, excess stress

HYPERTENSION

Blood pressure is the pressure the heart exerts to circulate blood in the body (measured in millimeters of mercury, mmHg). The value is given by two numbers: the systolic or maximum pressure and the diastolic or minimum pressure.

Systolic blood pressure is measured when the heart contracts and pumps blood through the arteries. Commonly called "maximum."

Diastolic blood pressure is measured between two contractions as the heart relaxes and fills with blood. Commonly called "minimum."

A blood pressure that does not exceed 130 mmHg for systolic and 80 mmHg for diastolic is considered desirable. The blood pressure value varies typically throughout the day: it increases in the morning, with effort, emotions, cold, or pain, and decreases with heat, rest, and sleep. We speak of hypertension when blood pressure exceeds the values of 140/90 mmHg, regardless of age and other concomitant pathological conditions. Hypertension develops when the walls of large-caliber arteries lose their natural elasticity and become stiff. And the smallest blood vessels constrict. Hypertension strains the heart, can increase its size, make it less efficient and promote atherosclerosis. For this reason, people with high blood pressure run a greater risk of heart attack or stroke. Hypertension can also cause kidney failure and damage eyesight.

CHOLESTEROLEMIA

Cholesterol is a molecule of the lipid (or fat) class that makes up the membrane of our cells. It is mainly produced by the liver and is used in the synthesis of some essential hormones, as well as playing a vital role in the production of vitamin D. In addition to the amount typically produced by the body, cholesterol can be introduced with the diet: it is present in foods rich in animal fats such as meat, butter, cured meats, cheeses, egg yolks, and offal. However, an excess of cholesterol, or hypercholesterolemia, in the blood can harm the heart, arteries, and brain. At the level of the streets, cholesterol can damage the internal lining of the vessels, giving rise to a series of degenerative phenomena: the walls of the vessels become more rigid. They become covered with "encrustations," i.e., atherosclerotic plaques. The plaques cause a narrowing of the ship, which hinders the passage of blood, or they cause abnormal dilations, i.e., aneurysms. If the coronary arteries (arteries to the heart) are affected, the risk of myocardial infarction is very high. Likewise, accumulation of cholesterol in the streets leading to the brain (carotids and their branches) predisposes to stroke. In smokers, the damage occurs mainly on the walls of the aorta, favoring the formation of an aneurysm or on the arteries of the lower limbs. However, it should be reiterated that the risk of cardiovascular disease depends on several factors. The damage done by cholesterol to the arteries, for example, is much more severe in those with hypertension. On the other hand, those with low blood pressure can live their entire lives with even higher levels of total cholesterol without significant consequences.

Conversely, those with acceptable cholesterol levels but blood pressure slightly higher than average values run more significant risks. Exposure to cardiovascular risk, therefore, increases not the presence of a single factor such as high cholesterol, hypertension, obesity, or diabetes but their sum.

DIABETES

Carbohydrates or sugars are essential among the nutrients we take in our diet, glucose being the most easily used by the body to produce energy. The pancreas produces a hormone, insulin, which facilitates the entry of glucose into the cells. However, people with diabetes do not produce insulin (type I diabetes), have little, or are unable to use it as they should (type II diabetes): this causes a rise in the blood glucose level, i.e., an increase in blood sugar. We speak of diabetes when the fasting blood sugar measured at least twice at an interval of one week is equal to or greater than 126 mg/dl. There are two forms of diabetes:

type 1 diabetes, or insulin-dependent diabetes, which affects about 10 percent of diabetic people, and which affects young people.

type 2, or non-insulin-dependent diabetes, affects about 90 percent of diabetic people and is very often linked to excess weight.

The causes of type I diabetes are essentially genetic. Type II diabetes depends on age, familiarity, and unhealthy habits, such as a sedentary lifestyle, a diet too rich in sugars, and obesity.

Diabetes is a significant disease that causes vascular complications in all districts, particularly in the coronary, carotid, and lower limbs arteries (macro-vascular damage) and in the streets of the eye, kidney, and nervous system peripheral (micro-vascular damage). Diabetic vascular disease is generally more widespread and severe than a non-diabetic subject and is very often calcified. It is a pathology equivalent to coronary artery disease for all intents and purposes. In this scenario, the coexistence of other risk factors, smoke first, becomes an explosive mixture.

OBESITY

Excess weight is the antechamber of several risk factors for heart disease, such as high cholesterol, hypertension, and diabetes. Excess pounds make the heart work excessively, even to perform everyday functions. A correct assessment of cardiovascular risk includes evaluating the body mass index (BMI, or BMI in Anglo-Saxon) and the measurement of the waistline. The body mass index is obtained through the formula weight (in kg)/height (in meters) squared: values between 25-29.9 describe a situation of overweight, while values above 30 configure a condition of obesity. The waist size represents the measurement of the circumference taken at the midpoint between the last rib and the crest of the hip (which generally corresponds to the navel line). This measurement should not exceed 94 centimeters for men and 80 centimeters for women. When the values exceed 103 cm for men and 88 cm for women, the probability of getting sick becomes high. Waist circumference is important because not all body fat is the same. In particular, the adipose tissue concentrated in the abdominal area seems mainly related to an increase in the probability of cardiovascular disease. Scientific evidence, in fact, shows that the distribution of fat in the body also counts for predicting cardiac risk: with the same body mass index, subjects with an "apple" body conformation, with an accumulation of visceral fat, are more exposed than those who have a "pear" body shape, with collections on the thighs and buttocks. Finally, the importance of the time factor should not be underestimated. Living with excess pounds for years or decades can negatively affect arterial and coronary health in adulthood.

SMOKE

In addition to the onset of tumors such as lung cancer, smoking is a significant cardiovascular risk factor, especially in young people. Smoking reduces the amount of oxygen reaching the heart, increases blood pressure and heart rate, damages the arteries by promoting vasoconstriction and spasm, and promotes atherosclerotic disease. All of this increases the likelihood of stroke or heart attack progression of lower extremity arterial disease and is the most critical risk factor for the formation and progression of abdominal aortic aneurysm. The Interheart study confirmed that smoking is one of the most important causes of non-fatal myocardial infarction, especially in young people (under 40). Smoking is harmful in every way - cigarettes, pipes, cigars, chewable tobacco - and the risk is closely related to the number of cigarettes smoked: 5 are less harmful than 20, but even with a few cigarettes, there is no zero risk.

Furthermore, passive smoking also increases the risk of cardiovascular diseases for those exposed, men or women, at home or in the workplace, of the degree of contact and the duration of exposure. Every year 8 million people die from diseases caused by tobacco consumption (1 person every 4 seconds). The life expectancy of a smoker is eight years less than that of a non-smoker. Yet it's never too late to quit, regardless of when you started and how much you smoke.

Quitting smoking extends life expectancy and reduces the onset of many diseases:

Those who stop smoking between the ages of 35 and 39 live on average, respectively, 5 and 3 years longer than their peers who continue to smoke; those who stop between the ages of 65 and 69 increase their life expectancy by an average of 1 year.

Blood pressure and heart rate decrease twenty minutes after the last cigarette. The risk of having a heart attack is reduced by 50% after 1 year.

From 5 to 15 years after quitting, the risk of stroke is reduced to the same level as that of a non-smoker.

After 15 years, the risk of coronary heart disease is similar to that of someone who has never smoked.

Quitting smoking also improves the quality of life: smell and taste improve after a few days, the skin becomes brighter again after a few weeks, the teeth become whiter and the breath more pleasant, the breathing improves, and the smoking cough disappears, you move more efficiently and, in general, you feel better and fitter.

CHAPTER 2: Foods to eat and avoid.

It has been known for some time that nutrition plays a fundamental role in preserving our health and hearts. Suffice it to say that the World Health Organization (WHO) has declared that 1/3 of cardiovascular diseases and cancer are preventable thanks to a healthy and balanced diet.

In fact, there are many allied foods for the health of our cardiovascular systems, such as fruit and vegetables, legumes, especially soy and whole grains, but also coffee, tea, red wine, dark chocolate, and vinegar of Apple.

But why are these foods considered "friends" of the heart? And in what quantities would it be better to consume them? Let's clarify with Dr. Andrew Carson, the nephrologist in charge of the clinical nutrition clinic of San Marco Polyclinic and nutritionist of Smart Clinic 'Le Due Torri.'

Nutrition and Heart Health: What's the Connection?

"The link between food and heart health is powerful. In fact, there are foods that, if consumed constantly and in the right quantities, play an important role in protecting the cardiovascular system and preventing the onset of arterial hypertension and diabetes mellitus, the increase in triglycerides, as well as "bad" cholesterol (LDL) versus 'good' (HDL).

In other words, they help reduce the risk of developing cardiovascular diseases, including heart attack and stroke", explains Carson.

Foods for the heart

"The well-being of the most important muscle in our body can be preserved with a diet that favors the intake of foods that contain specific and essential nutrients for the heart - underlines the specialist -. And it's not just important to choose the right type of food. A heart-friendly diet must also include consuming them in the correct doses. So, let's look at them specifically."

1 green leafy vegetable

Favor the consumption of green leafy vegetables such

as spinach, cabbage, zucchini, arugula, fennel, etc., because they are rich in vitamin K, which helps protect the arteries.

Furthermore, it is a source of nitrates which:

• reduce blood pressure.

• slow down the aging of the arteries.

• improve the functionality of the blood vessel lining.

The ideal would be to consume at least 1 portion of vegetables at lunch and dinner as a snack, in the form of smoothies, for example.

Fresh and dried fruit

Fresh fruit is a reserve of vitamins A, B1, B2, B3, and C, which protect the heart and arteries. For example, you should eat oranges, citrus fruits, mangoes, kiwis, plums, apricots, cherries, apples, melons, and pineapples. Greenlight is also for berries and red fruits (blueberries, raspberries, blackberries, currants, strawberries), which contain antioxidants (substances capable of counteracting, slowing down, or neutralizing free radicals) to help keep bad cholesterol and blood pressure under control sanguine. It is advisable to consume at least 3 servings every day. Also excellent are dried fruit such as walnuts, hazelnuts, and peanuts, rich in vitamin E and omega-3 fatty acids, which fight the increase in blood pressure and 'cleanse' the arteries of bad cholesterol. In this case, 10-15 grams of dried fruit per day is recommended.

Fish, especially the blue one

Oily fish such as mackerel, anchovies, etc., and salmon have a high content of omega-3 fatty acids, which reduce the risk of sudden cardiac death and the mortality rate due to heart disease. Therefore, eating it 3 or 4 times a week would be good.

Legumes

Chickpeas, lentils, beans, peas, and broad beans are a source of vegetable protein and macronutrients (fiber, carbohydrates) but are low in sugar and fat. Furthermore, legumes contain essential mineral salts:

iron, which decreases lousy cholesterol.

potassium, which reduces blood pressure.

phosphorus favors the proper functioning of the muscles and, therefore, the heart.

They should be put on the table possibly 2 or 3 times a week.

Soy

Soy is a legume with a high protein content, double that of meat. It is also rich in omega-3 fatty acids, which, as already mentioned, fight cardiovascular diseases. It is also in lecithins, a famous phosphorous substance with anti-cholesterol-reducing properties.

Soy is, therefore, able to keep blood triglycerides low and keep diabetes, another cardiovascular risk factor, under control.

The recommended dose is 1 serving daily, such as a 250 ml cup of soy milk, a soy yogurt, or a 100g stick of tofu.

Cereals are better if whole meal

Whole meal bread, pasta, rice, oats, rye, barley, buckwheat, and quinoa are all rich in fiber which can help reduce bad cholesterol. However, the important thing is to vary the choice of cereals, prefer whole grains and consume a small portion every day (about 70 grams).

Coffee and tea in moderation

Coffee and tea contain polyphenols, substances with antioxidant and anti-inflammatory properties, which can regulate the metabolism of lipids and glucose, keep cholesterol levels at bay and protect the cardiovascular system. However, it is essential not to exceed 2 cups of coffee/tea per day.

8. Red wine, as grandparents advised

Red wine is rich in resveratrol, a substance found in the skin of grapes, especially the black one, with antioxidant properties and can counteract lousy cholesterol and raise the levels of the good one. According to various studies, consuming 1 glass of red wine daily benefits the heart and the brain, reducing the risk of heart attack and stroke.

Chocolate, yes, but dark

Chocolate is a source of flavonoids, a subcategory of polyphenols, which promote the elasticity of blood vessels and reduce the risk of weight gain and the related harmful consequences on cardiovascular health. However, the important thing is that it is dark (at least 70% cocoa) and no more than 10 grams per day (a small square).

Vegetable oils and fats

To season dishes, go ahead with extra virgin olive oil containing oleic acid. This monounsaturated fat has protective effects on cardiovascular diseases. On the other hand, animal fats such as butter, lard, and vegetable oils such as palm oil, sauces, and condiments with high-fat content should be limited.

11. Apple cider vinegar

Recent studies have shown that consuming apple cider vinegar alone or in dishes would seem to positively affect the cardiovascular system's health. This is because it contains minerals such as phosphorus, sulfur, iron, magnesium, and calcium, essential for strengthening the heart and the body's immune defenses, and potassium, which affects the proper functioning of the heart and muscles.

It is also a source of pectin, a water-soluble fiber capable of protecting cells and blood vessels; it helps reduce the level of cholesterol in the blood, promotes the sense of satiety, and hinders the absorption of fats."

CHAPTER 3: The main bases of the heart diet

Improving the diet to help our heart health: a fundamental concept also for heart failure because correct lifestyles, starting with nutritional care and without neglecting moderate but regular physical activity, represent a cornerstone of secondary prevention, not only to prevent acute cardiovascular events but also to facilitate the recovery of those who are ill.

Suppose there is no perfect diet for heart failure. In that case, it is true, however, that especially for heart failure patients, the basic principles of a correct and balanced diet apply. This means setting up a diet that ensures a proper intake of fats, proteins, and carbohydrates by abolishing - or limiting as much as possible - sugary drinks and alcohol.

Heart health also passes from the table, and, for heart failure, it is essential to take care not only of the quality of the food but also of the correct quantities: consuming everything, but always in the right portion. Fortunately, in Italy, the Mediterranean diet also offers patients with heart failure an actual multiplicity of choices, which allow them to satisfy the taste and convivial pleasure of eating with a correct and balanced diet.

Especially for those suffering from heart failure, it is advisable to limit the intake of saturated fats, which are notoriously harmful to cardiovascular health. This means reducing meat consumption, especially red meat, sausages, eggs, or whole dairy products, while ensuring a balanced supply of proteins through fish, cereals, legumes, and many types of fruit and vegetables. Saturated fats can raise blood cholesterol, one of the most severe cardiovascular risk factors. Cholesterol tends to accumulate in the heart arteries, causing them to become progressively blocked, thus limiting blood flow to the heart muscle. This condition, known as atherosclerosis, can cause chest pain or cardiac arrest in cases of total obstruction. Atherosclerosis and coronary artery disease contribute significantly to the increase in blood pressure and, over time, to the onset of heart failure.

Pay attention to the consumption of salt. Excessive sodium consumption promotes fluid retention, further tiring the heart muscle. For this reason, patients with heart failure are advised to consume no more than 2 grams of sodium per day: more or less 5 grams of table salt, the equivalent of a teaspoon.

It is a result that can be obtained through various expedients, such as:

Choose foods or versions of foods that are low in sodium; give preference to fresh fruits and vegetables rather than processed foods; do not add salt when cooking; always read food labels at the time of purchase to check the sodium content. Bearing in mind that substances such as sodium glutamate (the main ingredient of bouillon cubes), sodium benzoate (present in sauces, condiments, and margarine), and sodium citrate (flavor enhancer in sweets, jellies, and drinks) always indicate the presence of additional salt content. Avoid alcoholic beverages. Alcohol is a toxic molecule, and excess, especially in the company of heart failure, can cause the heart to dilate and weaken. Unless there are severe symptoms, moderate consumption can include half a glass of wine per meal for men and one for women.

Limit your coffee consumption. Yes, to moderate caffeine consumption, no more than three coffees a day.

Don't overdo it with liquids. Fluid retention is a risk to avoid for those suffering from heart failure because it places a more significant workload on the heart. And the excess fluid can end up in the lungs, making breathing more difficult. The amount of liquids that can be taken daily varies from 1.5 to 2 liters. These quantities should be considered as water, tea, herbal teas, milk, and broth.

An ally called potassium. Many patients take diuretics prescribed to counteract water retention. However, these drugs can reduce potassium levels in the body, the main mineral present in cells.

Fundamental for muscle contraction, including that of the heart muscle, potassium helps regulate the balance of fluids and minerals inside and outside the cells and helps maintain normal blood pressure by dampening the effects of sodium. For this reason, patients with heart failure must supplement their diet with potassium-rich foods: bananas, apricots, plums, soybeans, melons, legumes, potatoes, and fish such as trout or cod.

An added value to counteract the risks of heart failure even at the table comes from the Heart Diet, much more than a simple list of foods but a natural lifestyle traditionally adopted in the southern regions of Italy. The benefits of the Heart Diet on cardiovascular health have been extensively investigated by researchers and many doctors; but why is the Hearth Diet so important for heart failure? Because it is a diet characterized by a high intake of fresh fruit and vegetables, cereals (especially unrefined), legumes, dried fruit (walnuts, almonds, hazelnuts); the primary source of fat is olive oil, used as a condiment; proteins are mainly supplied by fish, while cheeses and dairy products are consumed to a lesser extent; meat, especially red meat, is eaten occasionally.

The Heart Diet is also rich in antioxidant and anti-inflammatory substances, such as polyphenols, tocopherol, and phytosterols, which help to counteract oxidative stress and inflammation, involved in the process that leads to the formation of atherosclerotic plaques in the arteries and also boast antiplatelet properties which protect against the risk of thrombosis. Also important is the intake of fibers that contributes to the decrease in body weight, fat mass, and fasting blood sugar values, essential parameters to monitor in the event of heart failure. The high intake of dietary fiber also modifies intestinal bacterial flora. By decreasing the amount of choline and carnitine taken in the diet, the intestinal production of a substance (TMAO) is reduced, which has both a vascular inflammatory effect and a pro-thrombotic action.

It is essential to point out that the possible cardiovascular benefit is not linked to the intake of single foods but precisely to mixing the properties of all the nutrition present in the Mediterranean diet. Finally, a further benefit is obtained by associating moderate but constant physical exercise with the diet because it involves improvements in muscle strength and aerobic capacity, which are fundamental for all patients with heart failure.

CHAPTER 4: Causes and symptoms of heart disease.

For most of the symptoms that could be the alarm bell of heart problems, both the seemingly trivial ones and the potentially more dangerous ones, the story told by the patient is significant. Suppose the interested party manages to remain rational and identify the characteristic indicators of his disorder. In that case, he provides the cardiologist with a detailed description of the symptoms, which, for the attentive specialist, often assume greater importance than complex, prolonged, and sometimes annoying to the patient.

Dyspnea

A typical symptom of heart disease is shortness of breath or, in medical language, dyspnea. When a patient complains of shortness of breath, it is necessary to understand whether this symptom depends on a cardiac, respiratory or neurological, psychological, or metabolic problem (for example, anemia or thyroid disease). If accurate and detailed, the patient's account can offer reasonable indications. Dyspnea of cardiac origin generally occurs with physical effort or in a lying position (in this case, it is defined as orthopnea). The typical case is the patient who experiences shortness of breath after climbing a flight of stairs or an uphill journey or sleeps with two pillows to stay relieved and breathe better.

Cardiac dyspnea is usually linked to a functional deficit of the heart muscle, which can meet the body's needs at rest. Still, it is unable to supply it with enough blood in the event of increased requests, such as, for example, physical effort. The condition may occur in which the excess blood, not being able to be pushed to the lower part of the body, stagnates upstream of the heart, at the level of the lungs, and oozes inside the alveoli can cause a hazardous disease such as acute pulmonary edema. Cardiac dyspnea may most commonly be caused by valvular disease (e.g., mitral valve stenosis or regurgitation) or heart muscle disease (dilated cardiomyopathy, where the heart increases in size, sometimes as a result of a significant heart attack) or a lack of coronary blood circulation. In the latter case, dyspnea represents an anginal equivalent; this means that some patients, due to a narrowing of the coronary arteries, instead of accusing the classic chest pain we mentioned earlier, experience shortness of breath.

Syncope

Another significant disorder, also common to some heart diseases and neurological problems, is syncope, i.e., a sudden loss of consciousness not preceded by any warning (totally different from the "feeling of fainting" pervasive, especially in anxious people or suffering from low blood pressure).

Syncope can be due to valvular or heart muscle diseases (e.g., aortic stenosis and hypertrophic cardiomyopathy). Still, more frequently, it is linked to cardiac arrhythmia.

Two types of cardiac arrhythmia can cause sudden loss of consciousness:

bradycardia (i.e., a "block" that occurs at a point of the electrical circuit that crosses the heart to make it contract), which causes a pause in the heartbeat for a few seconds and the consequent lack of blood flow to the brain or, at the contrary,

ventricular tachycardia, i.e., a potentially very dangerous arrhythmia (it can, in fact, evolve spontaneously towards ventricular fibrillation and cardiac arrest) which consists of an accelerated beat that starts from the ventricles, so rapid and disordered that it does not allow the heart to fill adequately of blood and to pump it towards the brain, consequently bringing it a reduced blood flow and therefore of nourishment.

Even in the case of syncope, the patient's story is crucial to understanding whether the loss of consciousness may be due to one of the potentially lethal pathologies mentioned above or, more simply, to a drop in blood pressure or an anxiety attack or panic.

Palpitations

Finally, among the innumerable cardiac disorders, there is the vast chapter on "palpitations," which range from the sensation of "heart sinking" or "missing beat" typical of extrasystole to the palpitations sensation, which identifies a condition of accelerated heartbeat heart rate (or "tachycardia"). In this case, it is necessary to be able to evaluate whether it is a "sinus" tachycardia or a different form ("supraventricular" or "ventricular"). In the first case, the tachycardia is linked to a more incredible speed of the sinus node, i.e., of that structure which already usually acts as a cardiac "step marker" (as occurs in the case of physical effort, emotional stress, or in conditions of fever, anemia, hyperthyroidism, and other situations). In the second case, it is a condition in which a point of the heart different from the sinus node takes over and sends a more or less long series of electrical impulses to the rest of the seat until the sinus node resumes its typical sequence.

CHAPTER 5: American Heart Association (AHA) recommendations?

Ten rules for a healthy diet in defense of the heart. These are those proposed by the American Heart Association and published in recent days in Circulation, essentially based on some key concepts: focus on healthy dietary models rather than single foods; take care of nutrition at every stage of life; promote sustainable consumption from an environmental point of view; contrast phenomena that keep consumers away from correct eating habits. This is how the ten fundamental rules are proposed based on the most recent scientific evidence. First, balance calorie intake and consumption to maintain adequate body weight; then, abundant and varied consumption of fruit and vegetables is essential. Thirdly, I prefer whole foods, and fourthly, I resort to healthy protein sources, mainly of vegetable origin, with regular fish and seafood consumption, limiting that of red and processed meats. Fifth: ban tropical oils and partially hydrogenated fats from the table in favor of using vegetable oils. Minimize the consumption of processed foods and, seventh, foods or beverages with added sugars. Prefer low-salt foods; limit the consumption of alcohol and finally, always apply these rules, regardless of where the food is prepared or consumed. Diet and Sustainability For the first time, the theme of Sustainability appears in the AHA dietary guidelines. "Animal products and, in particular, red meat, have the greatest environmental impact in terms of water and soil consumption, contributing significantly to greenhouse gas emissions," the document reads. "Going therefore in the direction of a greater consumption of plant-based diets rather than animal-based guarantees, at the same time, benefits for individual health and the environment." With one caveat, though: Not all eco-sustainable diets are heart healthy. For example, suppose a plant-based diet includes a lot of refined carbohydrates and added sugars. In that case, it increases the risk of type 2 diabetes and heart disease. They are called "Life's Simple 7," and the American Heart Association has developed seven recommendations within everyone's reach that can save the heart and beyond, according to the data just presented during the annual congress of the US association. In fact, all health gains by changing the lifestyle according to the "Life's Simple 7": these are steps that are good for anyone, cost nothing, and are very effective for improving well-being and lengthening life expectancy. "Start by putting at least one or two into practice," the experts recommend. Perhaps, as Japanese research presented at the congress suggests, following simple advice like taking public transport to go to work: a good habit that can reduce weight, blood pressure, and blood sugar in one fell swoop

Keeping Blood Pressure Low High blood pressure is a significant risk factor for heart attacks and strokes. Keeping it within average values (80/120 mm Hg is considered ideal) reduces the effort that the heart, blood vessels, and kidneys must make for good Circulation. Not surprisingly, according to the data presented at the American Heart Association congress collected on about 7,000 people, those who follow the seven heart-saving rules also have a reduction in the risk of chronic kidney disease equal to 62 percent. Keep Cholesterol under control Cholesterol causes the formation of plaques in blood vessels which can then detach, clogging the arteries and causing heart attacks and strokes: measure the values and keep them below the permitted limits (the ideal is less than 200 milligrams of Cholesterol per deciliter of blood) is suitable for health. Suppose cholesterol control is associated with compliance with the other rules dictated by Americans. In that case, the risk of other chronic diseases, such as chronic obstructive pulmonary disease, is also reduced: the probability drops by 49 percent, according to the data collected. Reduce blood sugar An excess of sugar in the blood is detrimental to practically all organs, from the heart to the kidneys, from the eyes to the nervous system. It is, therefore, necessary to keep fasting blood glucose values below 110 milligrams per deciliter of blood;

glycated hemoglobin, indicative of the blood sugar trend in the last two-three months, should be below 5-6 percent in non-diabetics and remain below 7 percent in diabetics. Eating healthy is one of the most effective weapons to combat cardiovascular diseases, and not only, given that the data collected by Americans show that respecting the seven heart-saving rules also lowers the probability of tumors by 20 percent. The Mediterranean diet, rich in fruit, vegetables, whole grains, and legumes, is the best for keeping the heart not just in perfect shape. Lose weight. Being overweight harms the heart, lungs, vessels, and skeleton: it strains the body. It worsens all the other indices considered by the «Life's Simple 7». Therefore, maintaining a healthy weight is an excellent "life insurance, " as American cardiologists explain. Quit smoking Smokers have a greater risk of cardiovascular disease and endangering lung health: quitting is the wisest decision you can make for your well-being, as the Americans point out. Also, abandoning cigarettes, associated with other health-saving rules, reduces the probability of pneumonia by 43 percent. Physical activity A golden rule to be included in daily habits to improve length and quality of life: exercising regularly positively impacts all cardiovascular parameters and improves health in general. Going to work by public transport is not part of «Life's Simple 7. » Still, it is a simple recommendation to increase the level of physical activity: a study just presented at the congress of US cardiologists has, in fact, shown that going to the office by bus or the subway reduces the probability of being overweight by 44 percent, that of diabetes by 34 percent, and the risk of hypertension by 27 percent compared to those who choose the car. As explained by the authors, a group of researchers from the Horiuchi City Health Examination Center in Osaka, Japan, «Choosing public transport means making more movement on foot to move from the stop to your destination and should be considered as a simple and effective means of increase the level of daily physical exercise.

CHAPTER 6: Breakfast

Strawberry Smoothie

Total Time: 5 mins / **Prep. Time:** 5 mins /
Cooking Time: / **Difficulty:** Easy
Serving Size: 4 servings

Ingredients:
- 1 pound of strawberries
- 1/2 lemon
- 2 tablespoons of maple syrup
- a few mints leaves.
- 1 banana

Instructions:
In a large bowl, wash the strawberries, remove the green stalk, and cut them in half. Next, peel the banana and cut it into slices inside the bowl. Start extracting the juice from the strawberries and then continue with the banana. Combine the maple script and mint with the juice and mix. Place in the fridge and serve fresh.

Nutritional Values: Calories: 80 kcal /
Carbohydrates: 4 g / Proteins: 8 g / Fiber: 22 g /
Fats: 2 g

Colorful Vegetables and Muesli

Total Time: 15 mins / **Prep. Time:** 15 mins /
Cooking Time: / **Difficulty:** Easy
Serving Size: 4 servings

Ingredients:
- ½cucumber
- salt
- 3 oz. 5-grain cereal flakes
- 1 tbsp slivered almonds
- 1 yellow bell pepper (about 7 ounces)
- 3tomatoes (about 2.5 ounces)
- 2 sprigs basil
- 5 oz yogurt (low-fat)
- peppers

Instructions:
Rinse and dry the cucumber thoroughly. Cut in half lengthwise, remove the seeds with a teaspoon and cut cucumber into small cubes. Place diced cucumber in a bowl and sprinkle with salt. Mix with cereal flakes and set aside. Toast the almonds until golden in a dry skillet and let cool. Meanwhile, rinse the bell pepper, wipe dry, cut into quarters and remove seeds. Cut pepper into thin strips. Rinse tomatoes, cut out the stems and cut tomatoes into quarters. Remove seeds and cut tomatoes into thin strips. Combine tomato and pepper strips with the cucumber-cereal mixture. Rinse the basil and shake dry. Pluck basil leaves, set some aside and finely chop the rest. Stir chopped basil with the yogurt and season with a little pepper. Serve muesli with the yogurt, sprinkle with almonds, garnish with remaining basil and serve.

Nutritional Values: Calories: 114 kcal /
Carbohydrates: 25 g / Proteins: 12 g / Fiber: 9 g /
Fats: 3 g

Crustless Quiche

Total Time: 50 mins / **Prep. Time:** 10 mins
/ **Cooking Time:** 35 mins / **Difficulty:** Easy
Serving Size: 7 servings

Ingredients:
- 1 cup cooked ham diced.
- 1 cup zucchini shredded.
- 1 cup cheddar cheese shredded.
- 8 large eggs
- ½ cup heavy cream
- ½ teaspoon dry mustard
- salt & pepper to taste.

Instructions:
Preheat oven to 355 °F. Grease a 9" pie plate. Place zucchini on a paper towel and remove moisture. Mix ham, zucchini and cheddar cheese in a pie plate. Whisk eggs, cream and seasonings. Pour over ham mixture. Bake uncovered 35 minutes or until a knife inserted in the center comes out clean.

Nutritional Values: Calories: 114 kcal /
Carbohydrates: 20 g / Proteins: 24 g / Fiber:
10 g / Fats: 8 g

Kale Frittata

Total Time: 25 mins / **Prep. Time:** 10 mins
/ **Cooking Time:** 15 mins / **Difficulty:** Easy
Serving Size: 4 servings

Ingredients:

- 8 large organic eggs
- 2 oz. freshly grated Pecorino
- A pinch of Salt and black pepper
- 2 oz. extra-virgin olive oil
- 1 medium onion
- 1 ½ cup Kale
- 9 Tbsp pepperoni or thinly sliced Italian spicysalami, cut into ½-inch pieces.
- 1 garlic clove, minced.

Instructions

Preheat broiler. Whisk all the eggs, 1½ tablespoons cheese, ¼ teaspoon salt, and ¼ teaspoon pepper in large bowl. Heat olive oil in medium nonstick broiler-proof skillet over medium heat. Add onion and sauté until tender but not brown, about 8-10 minutes. Add Kale in 3 batches; toss until each begins to wilt before adding next. Sprinkle with salt and pepper. Sauté for 4 minutes. Increase heat to medium-high; add salami and garlic to skillet and stir 60 seconds. Add eggs to skillet; stir to distribute evenly. Reduce heat to medium-low, cover, and cook until eggs are almost set but still moist in center, about 3 minutes. Sprinkle remaining 1½ tablespoons cheese over top. Transfer frittata to broiler and cook for 90 seconds. Using flexible spatula, loosen frittata around edges. Slide frittata out onto platter. Serve warm or at room temperature.

Nutritional Values: Calories: 122 kcal / Carbohydrates: 16 g / Proteins: 15 g / Fiber: 12 g / Fats: 9 g

Avocado Fries

Total Time: 15 mins / **Prep. Time:** 10 mins / **Cooking Time:** 5 mins / **Difficulty:** Easy
Serving Size: 3 servings

Ingredients:
- Canola oil for frying
- 1/4 cup flour
- 1 tsp kosher salt
- 2 large eggs, beaten to blend.
- 1 1/2 cups panko
- 2 medium avocados

Instructions:

Preheat oven to 180 °F. In a medium saucepan, heat oil Meanwhile, mix flour with salt in a shallow plate. Add eggs and panko in separate shallow plates. Add the avocado slices with the remaining salt. Dip each slice in flour, remove excess. Immerse in egg, then panko to cover. Set on 2 plates in a single layer. Fry a piece of avocado slices at a time until deep golden, 45 seconds to 1.5 minutes. Transfer slices to a plate lined with paper towels. Keep warm in oven while cooking the rest of avocados. Season with salt and parmesan.

Nutritional Values: Calories: 95 kcal / Carbohydrates: 10 g / Proteins: 8 g / Fiber: 24 g / Fats: 4 g

Simple Oat Waffles

Total Time: 5 mins / **Prep. Time:** 5 mins / **Cooking Time:** / **Difficulty:** Easy
Serving Size: 4 servings

Ingredients:
- 2 Cups oats
- 1 1/4 Cups water
- 1 cup soymilk or almond milk
- 3 Tbsp. olive oil
- 1/2 tsp. salt

Instructions:
In a blend add oats with soymilk and olive oil. Add salt and water and blend all ingredients. In a preheated waffle iron, bake waffles according to manufacturer's instructions. Serve warm.

Nutritional Values: Calories: 100 kcal / Carbohydrates: 9 g / Proteins: 14 g / Fiber: 7 g / Fats: 6 g

Cereal Bar Snack

Total Time: 5 mins / **Prep. Time:** 5 mins / **Cooking Time:** / **Difficulty:** Easy
Serving Size: 4 servings

Ingredients:

- 4 tablespoons unsalted butter
- 1/4 cup light brown sugar
- 1/4 cup honey
- 1/2 teaspoon sea salt
- 1/8 teaspoon cinnamon
- 3 cups cereal
- 1/4 cup roasted unsalted almonds.
- 1/4 cup cranberries

Instructions:

Line with parchment paper so that it hangs out of the pan. In a bowl, combine cereal, almonds, and cranberries. In a small saucepan melt butter, sugar honey, salt and cinnamon on medium-high heat until it reaches a bubbling boil. Continue to stir for 60 seconds. The mixture will be frothy. Remove from heat and pour over cereal mixture. Stir until for 2 minutes. Press the cereal mixture into the prepared pan using your dampened fingers or a piece of wax/parchment paper. Press mixture until it is even and flat. Let it cool and harden (15-20 minutes). Lift out parchment paper from pan and cut into individual bars. Store in a container.

Nutritional Values: Calories: 80 kcal / Carbohydrates: 4 g / Proteins: 8 g / Fiber: 22 g / Fats: 2 g

Banana Pancakes

Total Time: 15 mins / **Prep. Time:** 5 mins / **Cooking Time:** 10 mins / **Difficulty:** Easy
Serving Size: 3 servings

Ingredients:

- 1 Banana
- 2 Eggs
- 1/2 cup of oatmeal

Instructions:

Put all ingredients into your blender and blend well for 35 seconds. It gets everything so smooth and makes breakfast super simple. You can get a great deal on refurbished blenders directly from Blended too. Cook your pancakes on a griddle heated to medium-high, cooking from for about 2-5 minutes on each side. Serve with real maple syrup, peanut butter, or your favorite sugar-free jam!

Nutritional Values: Calories: 80 kcal / Carbohydrates: 8 g / Proteins: 18 g / Fiber: 10g

/ Fats: 5 g

Banana Bran Muffins

Total Time: 5 mins / **Prep. Time:** 5 mins / **Cooking Time:** / **Difficulty:** Easy
Serving Size: 4 servings

Ingredients:

- 1 1/4 cups All-Bran Original cereal
- 1 cup milk
- 3 large overripe bananas
- 1 egg
- 1/2 cup packed brown sugar.
- 1/4 cup unsweetened applesauce
- 1 teaspoon vanilla extract
- 1.5 cups whole wheat flour
- 2 oz. cup cocoa
- A pinch of baking powder and baking soda
- 1 teaspoon of salt
- 4 oz. chocolate chips

Instructions:

Preheat oven to 335 °F. Line muffin pans with about 16 paper liners. In a medium bowl, combine cereal and milk. Let sit 3-4 minutes until soft. Add bananas to a large mixing bowl and mash with a whisk. Whisk in egg, brown sugar applesauce and vanilla. Whisk in flour, cocoa, baking powder, baking soda and salt to the bowl. Add softened bran and whisk just until combined. Stir in chocolate chips. Ladle into prepared muffin pans and bake for 35 minutes. Let cool to room temperature.

Nutritional Values: Calories: 100 kcal / Carbohydrates: 24g / Proteins: 14 g / Fiber: 8 g / Fats: 4 g

Breakfast Cups

Total Time: 50 mins / **Prep. Time:** 20 mins / **Cooking Time:** 30 mins / **Difficulty:** Easy
Serving Size: 6 servings

Ingredients:

- 3 medium potatoes peeled and grated.
- 6 strips bacon cooked crispy.
- 3 large eggs
- 2 tablespoons olive oil
- Nonstick spray or extra oil
- Salt and pepper

Instructions:
Peel and grate potatoes and submerge them in cold water for a minute to wash off extra starch. Drain potatoes and dry them well on a few paper towels. In a skillet add olive oil and put it over medium-high heat and add potatoes and a pinch of salt. Cook potatoes, stirring occasionally, until they are browned. Try to break up potatoes as they cook so they stay in separate strands. They should take 15 minutes to brown nicely. Meanwhile cook bacon in the oven at 300 °F until very crispy. Grease a 6-cup muffin tin well and divide potatoes between tins. Leave a well in the center of each tin and make sure potatoes go up the sides to form potato cups. Crumble bacon and add about a strip of bacon into each tin. Scramble eggs and divide eggs between tins. You shouldn't need a full egg for tins. Season cups with a pinch of salt and pepper and bake until eggs are cooked through, about 25 minutes. When eggs are cooked, run a knife around the outside of each cup and remove each one. Pray that they don't stick, but they might stick a bit!

Nutritional Values: Calories: 112 kcal / Carbohydrates: 10 g / Proteins: 24 g / Fiber: 9 g / Fats: 7 g

Protein Pancakes

Total Time: 10 mins / **Prep. Time:** 4 mins / **Cooking Time:** 6 mins / **Difficulty:** Easy **Serving Size:** 4 servings

Ingredients:
- 1 cup Old Fashioned Oats
- 1 teaspoon Cinnamon
- 1 scoop Vanilla Protein Powder
- 1 teaspoon Pure Vanilla Extract
- 1 cup Plain Greek Yogurt
- 1/3 cup Milk
- 2 tablespoons Granulated Sugar, or honey.
- 1 Egg
- 1/4 teaspoon Baking Powder

Toppings:
- Peanut Butter
- Fruit
- Pure Maple Syrup

Instructions:
Add all of the ingredients to a blender. Blend until smooth. Heat a large skillet or griddle to medium heat. Spray with non-stick spray. Pour about 1/4 cup of batter onto hot surface. Cook for 5 minutes until bubbles start to form. Flip, and cook for an additional 1 minute. Serve with desired toppings.

Nutritional Values: Calories: 88 kcal / Carbohydrates: 14 g / Proteins: 16 g / Fiber: 8 g / Fats: 4 g

Cheese and Vegetable Frittata

Total Time: 30 mins / **Prep. Time:** 10 mins / **Cooking Time:** 20 mins / **Difficulty:** Easy **Serving Size:** 6 servings

Ingredients:
- 1 tablespoon olive oil
- 1 small red bell pepper, diced.
- ½ onion
- 1A pinch of salt.
- 1 small zucchini
- 1.5 pounds baby spinach, kale, or arugula
- 4 fresh basil leaves
- 5 large eggs
- 1/2 cup finely grated Parmesan cheese.
- A pinch of black pepper
- 2 medium scallions thinly sliced.
- 4 tbsp. fresh goat cheese, crumbled.

Instructions:
Arrange a rack in the middle of the oven and heat to 380°F. Heat the oil in cast iron or oven-safe nonstick skillet over medium-high heat until shimmering. Add the bell pepper, onion, and salt, and sauté until slightly softened, about 10 minutes. Add the zucchini, spinach, and basil, and cook until wilted, about 3 minutes. Remove from the heat. Whisk the eggs, Parmesan, and pepper together in a medium bowl until the eggs are broken up. Pour into the skillet over the vegetables. Sprinkle with the scallions and goat cheese. Bake until the eggs are almost set, about 15 minutes. Turn the oven on to broil on high and broil until the top is set and light golden-brown, about 2 minutes more. Let cool 10 minutes before serving and slicing.

Nutritional Values: Calories: 120 kcal / Carbohydrates: 17 g / Proteins: 22 g / Fiber: 6 g / Fats: 8 g

Caramelized Peach Quinoa Breakfast Bowl

Total Time: 20 mins / **Prep. Time:** 5 mins / **Cooking Time:** 15 mins / **Difficulty:** Easy **Serving Size:** 3 servings

Ingredients:

* 1 cup quinoa
* 2 cup water
* 2 peaches (apples work, too!), diced
* 1/4 tsp. cinnamon
* 3 Tbsp. pure maple syrup, divided
* splash fresh lemon juice
* assorted toppings: nut butters, chia seeds, unsweetened vanilla almond milk, coconut sugar, etc.

Instructions:

Add diced peach to a small pot with 2 Tbsp. maple syrup, 1/4 tsp. cinnamon, lemon juice, and salt. Bring the mixture to a boil over low-medium heat, and cook, stirring frequently, until peaches are tender and have slightly caramelized. Remove from the pot with a slotted spoon and set aside. Add water and quinoa to the pot. Add a pinch of cinnamon and cook according to package instructions. When finished, remove excess water, and stir in an additional Tbsp. maple syrup. To assemble: Add quinoa to a bowl. Top with caramelized peaches and any desired toppings.

Nutritional Values: Calories: 77 kcal / Carbohydrates: 18 g / Proteins: 16 g / Fiber: 10 g / Fats: 2 g

Strawberry Sauce for Pancakes and Waffles

Total Time: 15 mins / **Prep. Time:** 5 mins / **Cooking Time:** 10 mins / **Difficulty:** Easy **Serving Size:** 2 servings

Ingredients:

* 2 cups hulled and chopped fresh strawberries
* 3 oz. sugar
* Water
* 1 teaspoon lemon juice fresh
* 3 teaspoons cornstarch

Instructions:

In a small bowl combine cornstarch with 1 oz. of water. In a saucepan, combine chopped strawberries, sugar, water, and add lemon juice with cornstarch/water slurry. Stir and bring to a simmer. Stirring often until thick and syrupy, about 7 minutes. Remove from heat, pour over pancakes, waffles, or ice cream, and enjoy!

Nutritional Values: Calories: 60 kcal / Carbohydrates: 12 g / Proteins: 10 g / Fiber: 10 g / Fats: 3 g

Bircher Muesli

Total Time: 3 hours/ **Prep. Time:** 3 hours / **Cooking Time:** / **Difficulty:** Easy **Serving Size:** 5 servings

Ingredients:

* 2 cups Bob's Red Mill Muesli
* 2 cups plain low-fat yogurt
* 1.5 cups low fat milk
* 1 apple (shredded)
* 2 tablespoons lemon juice
* fresh berries (optional garnish)

Instructions:

Place the Muesli with yogurt and milk in a medium bowl and add apple with lemon juice. Mix and cover with plastic wrap and refrigerate for 2-4 hours. In the morning or when you're ready to eat, serve with fresh berries and ejoy.

Nutritional Values: Calories: 80 kcal / Carbohydrates: 24 g / Proteins: 12 g / Fiber: 20 g / Fats: 3 g

Carrot Oatmeal Greek Yogurt Muffins

Total Time: 20 mins / **Prep. Time:** 10 mins / **Cooking Time:** 10 mins / **Difficulty:** Easy **Serving Size:** 3 servings

Ingredients:

* 1 1/4 cups all-purpose flour
* 1 cup old fashioned rolled oats
* 1 1/2 tsp baking powder
* 1/2 tsp baking soda
* 1 tsp ground cinnamon
* 1/4 tsp ground nutmeg
* A pinch salt
* 2 large eggs
* 1/2 cup plain Greek yogurt

- 1/4 cup maple syrup
- 1/4 cup coconut palm sugar
- 1/4 cup unsweetened almond milk
- 3 tsp vanilla extract
- 4 oz. grated carrot
- 1/2 cup raisins (optional)

Instructions:

Preheat your oven to 340 °F and prepare a muffin pan by lining the cavities with paper liners or greasing them with cooking spray or oil. In a large mixing bowl, combine the flour, oats, baking powder, baking soda, cinnamon, nutmeg and salt. Mix. In a separate bowl, beat the eggs for 45-60 seconds and add yogurt, maple syrup, sugar, almond milk, and vanilla. Mix until well combined before folding in the grated carrots. Add the wet ingredients to the dry ingredients, mixing gently until just combined. Add raisins, if you love. Divide the batter evenly among the 10-14 muffin cups, filling almost to the top. Bake for 25-30 minutes. Allow the muffins to cool in the pan for 7 minutes and then transfer them to a wire rack to cool. Store in an airtight container at room temperature for up to 3-6 days.

Nutritional Values: Calories: 100 kcal / Carbohydrates: 14 g / Proteins: 19 g / Fiber: 24 g / Fats: 6 g

Baking Mix Soft Molasses Cookies

Total Time: 25 mins / **Prep. Time:** 5 mins / **Cooking Time:** 20 mins / **Difficulty:** Easy
Serving Size: 5 servings

Ingredients:

- 1/2 cup butter softened
- 4 ounces reduced-fat cream cheese softened
- 1/2 cup brown sugar
- 1 egg
- 1/2 cup molasses
- 2.5 cups baking mix
- 1 teaspoon ground cinnamon
- 1 tablespoon finely chopped crystallized ginger (or 1 teaspoon ground ginger)
- 1/4 cup dusting sugar optional

Instructions:

Preheat oven to 330 °F. Line 2 baking sheets with parchment paper. Mix butter, cream cheese, and sugar with an electric mixer on medium-low or vigorously by hand. Mix in egg and molasses on low until smooth. Add baking mix, cinnamon, and ginger, and stir until well combined. Use a medium dasher to scoop balls of dough two inches apart on baking sheet. Drop a pinch of dusting sugar on top of each cookie. Bake in preheated oven for 15-20 minutes. Halfway through baking, use a spoon to press the cookies down in the center into a flatter shape. Cool cookies on baking rack before storing.

Nutritional Values: Calories: 110 kcal / Carbohydrates: 24 g / Proteins: 9 g / Fiber: 9 g / Fats: 6 g

Garlic Drop Biscuits

Total Time: 30 mins / **Prep. Time:** 10 mins / **Cooking Time:** 20 mins / **Difficulty:** Easy
Serving Size: 4 servings

Ingredients:

- 2.5 cups all-purpose flour
- 1 oz. baking powder
- A pinch of salt and garlic powder
- 4 oz. unsalted butter
- ½ pound cheddar cheese
- 8 oz. of cold milk.

Butter Topping:
- 2.5 oz butter melted
- A pinch garlic powder
- 1 teaspoon salt

Instructions:

Preheat oven to 375 °F. Line a baking sheet with parchment paper. In a bowl add flour with salt, baking powder and garlic powder. Mix for 20 seconds. Cut the butter in the flour mixture just crumbly. Add cheese and mix. Add milk and mix again. Drop biscuits in the prepared pan. Mix butter with garlic and a pinch of salt in a bowl. Brush now on top of each roll. Bake for 15-20 minutes. Brush more butter on top and serve.

Nutritional Values: Calories: 94 kcal / Carbohydrates: 25 g / Proteins: 12 g / Fiber: 6 g / Fats: 8 g

Easy Pancakes

Total Time: 15 mins / **Prep. Time:** 5 mins / **Cooking Time:** 10 mins / **Difficulty:** Easy
Serving Size: 3 servings

Ingredients:
- 1 cup self-rising flour
- 2 Tbsp caster sugar
- 1 egg, lightly beaten
- ½ cup lemonade

Instructions:
In a bowl, combine the self-rising flour and caster sugar. Make a well in the dry mix and add the egg and lemonade. Gently mix the ingredients until well combined. In a pan over medium heat, add a knob of butter. Pour the desired amount of mixture into the pan. Roughly 1/4 cup mixture per pancake. Cook on one side until the mix starts to firm up, then flip the pancake and cook until done. Repeat steps until you use up all the mixture. Serve & Enjoy.

Nutritional Values: Calories: 100 kcal / Carbohydrates: 32 g / Proteins: 17 g / Fiber: 5 g / Fats: 6 g

Breakfast Sausages with Bell Peppers

Total Time: 5 mins / **Prep. Time:** 5 mins / **Cooking Time:** / **Difficulty:** Easy
Serving Size: 4 servings

- Ingredients:
- 4 sausages
- 2 bell peppers (med)
- 1 medium onion
- 3 scallions
- 1/4 teaspoon Spanish pimentón (smoked hot paprika)
- 1 teaspoon veg oil
- 1 clove garlic
- 3 sprigs thyme
- 1/4 scotch bonnet pepper (optional)
- pinch salt
- 1/4 teaspoon black pepper

Instructions:
Heat the veg oil on a low flame and add the sausages. TIP. add about 1/2 cup water to the pan so the sausages cook before they start burning on the outside before the inside in cooked or you can also place a lid on the pan. By the time the water burns off, your sausages should be close to being fully cooked. Now turn up the heat to fully 'brown' them on the outside. Takes about 20 minutes or so, depending on the thickness of them. Remove the now cooked sausages and set aside. Then add the garlic (crushed) and onion (chopped) to the same pan and cook on low for about 3 minutes. Then go in with the thyme, black pepper, salt, scotch bonnet and pimentón. Stir well and cook for a minute. It's now time to add the chopped bell peppers and scallions to the mix and stir well. The goal is to pick up all the flavors from the bottom of the pan from when we cooked the sausages. Let it go for about 2-3 minutes, so the peppers soften up a bit, but retain a bit of texture. The sausages should be cool by now, so chop into bite sized pieces and add to the pan.
Be: 4 g / Proteins: 8 g / Fiber: 22 g / Fats: 2 g

Pomegranate Banana Smoothie

Total Time: 5 mins / **Prep. Time:** 5 mins / **Cooking Time:** / **Difficulty:** Easy
Serving Size: 2w servings

Ingredients:
- ¼ cup almonds
- 1 medium banana
- 1 grapefruit (juiced)
- 1 medium pomegranate (just seeds)
- 1 oz unflavored sun warrior protein powder

Instructions:
Add the smoothie ingredients to a blender and blend with as much ice and water as you like, enjoy!

Nutritional Values: Calories: 65 kcal / Carbohydrates: 10 g / Proteins: 3 g / Fiber: 15 g / Fats: 0 g

Simple Egg Salad Sandwich

Total Time: 5 mins / **Prep. Time:** 5 mins / **Cooking Time:** / **Difficulty:** Easy
Serving Size: 8 servings
- Ingredients:

- 6 large, boiled eggs
- 1 Tbsp. Lemon Juice
- 1/3 cup Mayonnaise
- 1.5 tbsp mustard
- A pinch of salt and pepper
- ½ cups finely chopped Celery
- ¼ cup sliced green onions
- 8 slices rustic wheat bread
- 4 lettuce leaves

Instructions:

Chop the eggs and mix Mayonnaise with lemon Juice, salt and pepper in a bowl. Add eggs with celery with green onions and mix well. Refrigerate and serve on wheat bread with lettuce leaves. Enjoy

Nutritional Values: Calories: 142 kcal / Carbohydrates: 14 g / Proteins: 21 g / Fiber: 18 g / Fats: 12 g

Healthy Pancakes

Total Time: 15 mins / **Prep. Time:** 5 mins / **Cooking Time:** 10 mins / **Difficulty:** Easy **Serving Size:** 3 servings

Ingredients:
- 1 Banana
- 1 Egg
- 5 tbsp. Oat Flour
- 1 teaspoon Baking Powder

Instructions:
Add your favorite ingredients to the top, or Greek yogurt, fruit, jam, maple syrup, or a drizzle of honey. Mix ingredients in a deep dish and using a spoon, pour part of the mixture into a hot pan. Cook for 5 minutes per side and serve with your favorite dressing

Nutritional Values: Calories: 103 kcal / Carbohydrates: 32 g / Proteins: 13 g / Fiber: 6 g / Fats: 3 g

Peanut Butter Protein Overnight Oats

Total Time: 8 hours / **Prep. Time:** 5 mins /

Cooking Time: / Difficulty: Easy
Serving Size: 2 servings

- Ingredients:
- ½ cup soymilk or other plant-based milk
- ½ cup old-fashioned rolled oats
- 1 tablespoon pure maple syrup
- 2 teaspoons chia seeds
- 3 teaspoons powdered peanut butter
- A pinch of salt
- ½ banana

Instructions:
Stir soymilk (or other milk) salt, oats, syrup and mix well. Add then chia, powdered peanut butter and salt together jar. Refrigerate for 4 hours, better overnight. Serve topped with banana or berries if you like. Enjoy.

Nutritional Values: Calories: 100 kcal / Carbohydrates: 24 g / Proteins: 31 g / Fiber: 15 g / Fats: 6 g

Baked Oatmeal Muffins

Total Time: 1 hour / **Prep. Time:** 10 mins / **Cooking Time:** 40 mins / **Difficulty:** Easy **Serving Size:** 4 servings

Ingredients:
- 2 eggs
- 1 mashed banana
- 1/2 cup brown sugar
- 1 Tbsp. vanilla extract
- 1/2 tsp. salt
- 1/2 tsp. nutmeg
- 1 tsp. cinnamon
- 2 tsp. baking powder
- 3 cups oatmeal
- 1 cup half and half
- 1 cup chocolate chips

Instructions:
Preheat oven to 320 °F. Spray a muffin pan with non-stick spray. Add the eggs, mashed banana, brown sugar, vanilla extract, salt, cinnamon, and nutmeg to a large bowl. Mix together. Add the baking powder and oatmeal to the bowl and mix. Pour the half and half into the bowl and mix.
Fold in the chocolate chips. Add the mixture to the muffin pan. Bake for 35-40 minutes or until muffins are golden brown and no longer wiggle. Allow the muffins to cool for at least 20minutes to set up

Nutritional Values: Calories: 95 kcal / Carbohydrates: 35 g / Proteins: 12 g / Fiber: 9 g / Fats: 4 g

Mediterranean Breakfast Sandwich

Total Time: 20 mins / **Prep. Time:** 5 mins / **Cooking Time:** 15 mins/ **Difficulty:** Medium **Serving Size:** 2 servings

Ingredients:
- 2 tablespoons Basil Pesto
- 1 fresh Ciabatta roll, halved
- 1/3 tablespoon extra-virgin olive oil
- 2 eggs whites, beaten
- 1 small handful baby spinach
- 2 slices plum tomato
- 1 mozzarella cheese, 1/3-inch sliced
- Salt and pepper to taste

Instructions:
Preheat oven to 350 °F. Place Ciabatta roll on a baking sheet and toast in oven until edges are light brown and crispy for 10 minutes. Remove roll, brush with pesto and set aside on a plate.
Meanwhile in a large skillet heat the olive oil over medium heat. Pour in egg whites and season with salt and pepper. Cook until done about 5 minutes, flipping once. Place tomato slices on the bottom half of the Ciabatta, then egg (folding in half if necessary), cheese, spinach, and then place other half of roll-on top.

Nutritional Values: Calories: 110 kcal / Carbohydrates: 19 g / Proteins: 18 g / Fiber: 14 g / Fats: 8 g

Banana Oatmeal

Total Time: 35 mins / **Prep. Time:** 10 mins / **Cooking Time:** 25 mins / **Difficulty:** Easy **Serving Size:** 2 servings

Ingredients:
- 2 medium bananas
- 1.5 cups oatmeal
- 1/3 cup mini chocolate chipsInstructions:

Preheat oven to 320 °F. Line a baking sheet with cooking spray. Mash bananas in a bowl with a fork. Add oats and stir until all of the oats and bananas are mixed together; mix slowly. Sprinkle in the chocolate chips and mix again. Scoop one heaping tablespoon of the dough into your hands and free form into a cookie. Place on cookie sheet and continue just forming 8-14 cookies. Bake 20-25 minutes or until set through and lightly golden. Cool and enjoy!

Nutritional Values: Calories: 106 kcal / Carbohydrates: 25 g / Proteins: 19 g / Fiber: 10 g / Fats: 5 g

French Apple Tarte

Total Time: 30 mins / **Prep. Time:** 15 mins / **Cooking Time:** 15 mins / **Difficulty:** Medium **Serving Size:** 6 servings

Ingredients:
- Sweet Short crust Pastry
- 1/2 cup Butter
- 2 tbsp Powdered Sugar
- 1 Egg
- 1/3 cup + 2 tbsp Almond Meal
- 1 pinch Salt
- 1 1/3 cup Plain Flour
- Apple Tart Filling
- 11 oz Applesauce
- 3 large Apples
- 2 tbsp Lemon Juice

Instructions:
Cream the soft Butter and Powdered Sugar in the bowl of your mixer for about 5 minutes or until pale and fluffy. Mix in the Egg, Almond Meal and Salt until combined. Mix in the Flour on the lowest speed and stop as soon as the dough comes together to avoid overworking the pastry. Place the pastry between two sheets of baking paper and roll into a thin circle, larger than your tart pan. Place over a flat tray in the fridge to rest for at least 45-60 minutes, then line your tart pan with the pastry. Prick the bottom with a fork and place back in the fridge to rest for 30 minutes to 1 hour. Preheat your oven on 350 °F. While the over is preheating, place the pastry in the freezer. Blind bake for 10-15 minutes, or until the pastry is dry to the touch. Set aside to cool down

completely. Thinly slice the Apples, using a Mandoliner or a sharp knife. Place in a tray with the Lemon Juice and mix with your fingers to insure there is lemon juice all over the sliced apples. Fill the pastry crust with the Applesauce, using a spatula or the back of a spoon to spread it evenly. Place the sliced apples in circle over the applesauce, starting from the edges and finishing in the center of the tart. Bake for another 10 minutes, just to soften up the apple slices.

Nutritional Values: Calories: 150 kcal / Carbohydrates: 36 g / Proteins: 13 g / Fiber: 6 g / Fats: 10 g

Heart Healthy Overnight Oats

Total Time: 6.5 hours / **Prep. Time:** 30 mins / **Cooking Time:** / **Difficulty:** Easy
Serving Size: 4 servings

- Ingredients:
- 1/4 cup organic oats
- 1/2 teaspoon cinnamon
- 1/3 teaspoon pure vanilla extract
- 2 tablespoons flax seeds
- 1 tablespoon unsweetened shredded coconut
- 1 tablespoon of sliced almonds
- 1/3 cup almond milk
- 1/3 cup Greek yogurt

Instructions:
In a medium size bowl, mix the oats, yogurt, cinnamon, flax seeds, coconut and almonds.
Pour in the almond milk and blend well. Seal the bowl with a lid or plastic wrap or make individual mason jars filled for breakfast on the go. Refrigerate (soak) for 6 hours. Garnish with fresh berries and Fage Greek Yogurt and a dollop of the fruit from the yogurt container.

Nutritional Values: Calories: 101 kcal / Carbohydrates: 32 g / Proteins: 20 g / Fiber: 10 g / Fats: 6 g

Sauce Rustic Marinara

Total Time: 45 mins / **Prep. Time:** 15 mins / **Cooking Time:** 30 mins / **Difficulty:** Easy
Serving Size: 4 servings

Ingredients:

- 1 28- ounce can whole tomatoes San Marzano tomatoes
- 3 tablespoons extra-virgin olive oil
- 3 cloves garlic, finely chopped
- 1/2 cup finely chopped onion
- 1 tablespoon butter
- 1/4 teaspoon salt
- 1/2 teaspoon black pepper
- 4-5 fresh basil leaves, thinly sliced

Instructions:
Sauté the onion and garlic in the olive oil over medium heat until for 7 minutes. Don't let the garlic get too brown or it will be bitter. Add the tomatoes and break them up with your fingers. You can leave them as chunky as you like, or even chop them up if you prefer a smoother sauce. Add the salt, pepper, and butter and gently simmer for 20 minutes. Taste and adjust seasonings. Add a pinch of sugar to balance it out. Stir in the basil. Serve immediately.

Nutritional Values: Calories: 70 kcal / Carbohydrates: 10 g / Proteins: 9 g / Fiber: 4 g / Fats: 7 g

Hearty Bolognese Sauce

Total Time: 30 mins / **Prep. Time:** 10 mins / **Cooking Time:** 20 mins / **Difficulty:** Easy
Serving Size: 6 servings

- Ingredients:
- onion, finely diced
- 1 carrot, finely diced
- 6 cremini mushrooms, finely diced
- 8 oz eggplant, finely diced
- 10 oz tempeh, crumbled
- 3 cloves garlic, minced
- 1 cup sun-dried tomatoes, minced
- ¼ cup red wine vinegar
- 1 cup low-sodium vegetable broth or water
- 1 teaspoon dried oregano
- 1 teaspoon dried thyme
- 12 oz tomato sauce or strained tomatoes, no salt added

Instructions:
In a large sauté pan or skillet over medium heat add the onion, carrot, mushrooms and eggplant. Sauté for 3 minutes. Add the tempeh, garlic, sun-dried tomatoes, red wine vinegar, vegetable broth, tomato sauce and dried herbs. Stir well to combine, cover and simmer for 15 minutes until the eggplant is soft. Stir occasionally for even cooking and to prevent vegetables from sticking to the pan. Add more wine or water if needed. Serve over whole grain or legume pasta or spiralized vegetables

Nutritional Values: Calories: 90 kcal / Carbohydrates: 24 g / Proteins: 6 g / Fiber: 2 g / Fats: 8 g

Garlic Alfredo Sauce

Total Time: 10 hours / **Prep. Time:** 10 mins / **Cooking Time:** 10 mins / **Difficulty:** Easy
Serving Size: 4 servings

Ingredients:

- 1 medium white onion, chopped
- 4 large garlic cloves, minced
- 1-2 cups vegetable broth
- 1/2 Cup Cashews
- 4 tbsp Nutritional Yeast
- 1/4 tsp. Black Pepper
- 1/2 tsp. Salt
- 1 tbsp. Lemon Juice

Instructions:
Soak cashews overnight if you don't have a high-powered blender. Add one cup of the broth and onion to a large pan over medium-low heat. Add garlic after 3 minutes and cook for about 8 more minutes until onion is very tender, and the broth has evaporated. Put the onion and garlic into a blender with ¾ cup of remaining broth. Add the rest of the ingredients and blend on high until very creamy and smooth. Add more broth to reach desired consistency, and more salt and pepper if desired. Serve over preferred whole-grain pasta. Add lemon zest and parsley if loved.

Nutritional Values: Calories: 85 kcal / Carbohydrates: 28 g / Proteins: 10 g / Fiber: 3 g / Fats: 5 g

Spicy Salsa Meatloaf

Total Time: 1 hour/ **Prep. Time:** 10 mins /
Cooking Time: 45 mins / **Difficulty:** Easy
Serving Size: 8 servings

Ingredients:
- 2 pounds lean ground beef
- 1 jar salsa 15 ounces, choose your heat
- 1 white onion diced, medium-sized
- 1 cup breadcrumbs
- 1 egg beaten
- 1 teaspoon salt
- 1/2 teaspoon cayenne pepper
- Guacamole on the side

Instructions:
Preheat oven to 375 °F. Combine all ingredients into a large bowl and mix thoroughly. Move the mix into a meatloaf pan and spread evenly throughout the pan. Bake the meatloaf for 45 mins. Pull from oven and let the meatloaf rest for 5 minutes prior to cutting. Serve with guacamole on the side.
    Nutritional Values: Calories: 100 kcal / Carbohydrates: 26 g / Proteins

Baked Beans From Scratch

Total Time: 5 hours / **Prep. Time:** 10 mins /
Cooking Time: 4.5 hours/ **Difficulty:** Easy
Serving Size: 8 servings

Ingredients:
- 5 slices Bacon
- 1/2 whole Large Onion, Diced
- 2 cloves Garlic, Minced
- 1-pound Dried Great Northern Beans, Soaked
- 3 cups Water
- 1/2 cup Ketchup
- 1/4 cup Brown Sugar Or To Taste
- 2 tablespoons Molasses
- 1 tablespoon Apple Cider Vinegar
- 2 teaspoons Smoked Paprika
- 1/2 teaspoon Dijon Mustard
- 1/2 teaspoon Salt or To Taste
- 1/2 teaspoon Granulated Garlic

Instructions:
In a large pot add bacon, onion and garlic. Sauté over medium heat until bacon is brown, and onion has caramelized. Add all remaining ingredients to pan and bring to a simmer. Reduce heat and cook for 4.5 hours covered, until beans are thickened. Stir

as needed. Serve.

Nutritional Values: Calories: 104 kcal / Carbohydrates: 32 g / Proteins: 12 g / Fiber: 9 g / Fats: 5 g

Caramelized Pork Loin

Total Time: 2.5 hours/ **Prep. Time:** 30 mins /
Cooking Time: 2 hours / **Difficulty:** Hard
Serving Size: 10 servings

Ingredients:
Apple Filling
- 4 oz. butter
- 2 oz. brown sugar
- A pinch cinnamon
- 2 large apples

Pork Loin
- 55 oz. pork loin
- A pinch salt
- 1 tbsp. pepper
- 1 oz. vegetable oil
- 4 oz. orange juice
- 2 teaspoons brown sugar

Instructions:
Preheat the oven to 340 °F. Heat butter in a skillet. Add sugar with cinnamon and apples (diced). Mix Apples in melted butter and sugar. Cook over medium heat for 6 minutes just to caramelize in 1 side. Caramelize other sides (about 60-120 seconds). Cool them. Slice the pork loin down the center without cutting through the meat. When opened the 2 halves resample like a butterfly. Now, use a meat tenderizer and pound it flat. This operation will make it even easier to stuff and then cook the meat (if necessary). Add cooled cooked apples down the center and then bring the two sides of meat up around apple stuffing. In a small bowl mix salt and pepper; then season the meat. Now heat the oil in a skillet over high heat and sear the pork well on all sides. Transfer the pork into a large oven pot. Now add the orange juice and mix it with the sugar. Then pour it over the stuffed meat. Cook for an hour and a half or two, depending on how tender the meat is. Typically, pork needs to be roasted for about 20-25 minutes per pound (or 400 g), so you should adjust your cooking time accordingly depending upon the size of your pork. Internal temperature of at least **155°F** when tested with a cooking thermometer. When done cooking, remove the pork loin from the oven, wrap it in foil, and let it sit for a full 10 minutes before slicing. Resting is a very important step that helps

to keep the pork juicy and from drying out. **Serve and enjoy.**

Nutritional Values: Calories: 144 kcal / Carbohydrates: 32 g / Proteins: 26 g / Fiber: 14 g / Fats: 8 g

Sauce with Cranberries

Total Time: 3 hours / **Prep. Time:** 10 mins / **Cooking Time:** 15 mins/ **Difficulty:** Easy
Serving Size: 5 servings

Ingredients:
- 8 oz Fresh Cranberries
- 1/2 Cup Honey
- 3 Tbsp Light Brown Sugar
- 2 Cinnamon Sticks
- 5 Cloves (whole)
- 1/4 tsp - Nutmeg
- 1 Cup - Water

Instructions:
In a medium saucepan over medium heat combine all of the ingredients. Cook for some minutes and bring to a boil, reduce the heat to medium and cover stirring occasionally for 15 minutes. Remove lid and let simmer 2-3 more minutes or until thickened. Let thoroughly cool, then refrigerate 2-3 hours or overnight.

Nutritional Values: Calories: 104 kcal / Carbohydrates: 38 g / Proteins: 14 g / Fiber: 11 g / Fats: 4 g

Homemade Collagen Bone Broth

Total Time: 12 hours / **Prep. Time:** 20 mins / **Cooking Time:** 11 hours / **Difficulty:** Medium
Serving Size: 4 servings

Ingredients:
- 1 oz. ghee
- 3 medium carrots
- 3 stalks celery
- 4 cups assorted beef marrow bones
- 1 fresh bouquet garni
- 1 oz. apple cider vinegar
- 8 oz. Collagen Protein per liter of broth
- Salt to taste

Instructions:
In a non-stick pan sauté carrots and celery for a 3-5 minutes. Add the beef bones and continue to cook for 60 seconds. Add now bouquet garni and cover with water. Heat for 5 minutes and add the apple cider vinegar to the water. Simmer on a low heat for anywhere between 9-13 hours. Remove the bones and strain the vegetables out. Add the collagen (if using) for the amount of broth and stir until dissolved. Serve.

Nutritional Values: Calories: 79 kcal / Carbohydrates: 6 g / Proteins: 25 g / Fiber: 14 g / Fats: 6 g

Stock Of Chicken

Total Time: 4 hours / **Prep. Time:** 30 mins / **Cooking Time:** 3.5 hours / **Difficulty:** Medium
Serving Size: 12 servings

Ingredients:
- 10 lb. bag frozen chicken legs with thigh
- 4 medium yellow onions, quartered, skins on
- 4 stalks celery, cut in large pieces
- 4 carrots, split lengthwise, cut in large pieces
- 4 sprigs thyme
- 8 – 10 black peppercorns
- 4 – 6 bay leaves, depending on size
- 4 sprigs fresh parsley or 1 teaspoon dried parsley
- water, to cover

Instructions:
Open bag of chicken, empty contents into large stock pot. Wrap herbs in cheese cloth, tie with cotton string. Add all other ingredients. Cover with water by 2 inches. cover pot, bring to a boil.
Reduce heat to simmer. Simmer for 3.5 hours. Turn off heat. Use tongs to remove chicken one piece at a time. Remove skin and fat, discard. Remove meat, set aside, discard bones. Discard Bouquet Garni when you find it. When you've picked out all you can with the tongs, pour remaining contents through a colander. Save the good stuff, discard the rest. Shred chicken and place 2 cups at a time in sandwich size zip lock bags, freeze. scour the pot clean and return the stock. Let cool then chill overnight. Next morning remove congealed fat with a spatula. Reduce or not as you see fit. Place 2 cups at a time in sandwich sized zip lock bags, freeze.

Nutritional Values: Calories: 104 kcal /

Carbohydrates: 38 g / Proteins: 26 g / Fiber: 5 g / Fats: 8 g

Instant Pot Roast Beef and Gravy

Total Time: 150 mins / **Prep. Time:** 30 mins / **Cooking Time:** 90-100 mins / **Difficulty:** Medium
Serving Size: 8 servings

Ingredients:
- 3 lb. chuck roast beef not frozen
- A pinch salt and pepper
- 1 oz. olive oil
- 1/2 large onion sliced
- 2 cloves garlic finely chopped
- 1-2 teaspoons Montreal Steak Spice
- 3 bay leaves
- 1.5 lbs. chicken broth low sodium
- 2 teaspoons soy sauce
- 1 oz. red wine
- 1 cup quartered
- 2 carrots chopped
- 1.5 lb. golden baby potatoes
- 2 oz. cornstarch mixed with 4-6 tablespoons of cold water

Instructions:
Pat dry chuck roast beef with paper towels. Season with salt and pepper on both salt. Preheat olive oil in a fry pan. Add chuck roast and sauté until brown color, about 8-11 minutes per side. After, remove steak onto a plate, then add 1 sliced onion and sauté until softened about 6 minutes. Next add 3 finely chopped garlic cloves, Montreal Steak Spice, 2 bay leaves and sauté for 90-120 seconds. Pour in chicken broth, soy sauce, red wine, taste and season with salt and pepper, if needed. Return steak back into pan. Cover with a lid and cook for 60 minutes. Stir occasionally. Open the lid and remove steak onto a plate, slice it and cover with foil paper. Add vegetables and cover the lid and cook for 5 minutes. Transfer cooked vegetables onto a large serving plate and top it off with sliced beef roast. In a small dish mix cornstarch with water, then pour it into pan with broth. Bring it to a boil and cook for 60 seconds. Pour gravy over beef roast with vegetables and garnish with finely chopped parsley. Enjoy!

Nutritional Values: Calories: 119 kcal / Carbohydrates: 12 g / Proteins: 38 g / Fiber: 12 g / Fats: 10 g

CHAPTER 8: Sides

Grilled Asparagus

Total Time: 15 mins / **Prep. Time:** 5 mins / **Cooking Time:** 10 mins / **Difficulty:** Easy
Serving Size: 3 servings

Ingredients:
- 1 pound asparagus
- 1 tablespoon olive oil
- salt and pepper to taste

Instructions:
Preheat grill to medium-high heat. Season asparagus with olive oil, salt, and pepper. Grill for 5-10 minutes until tender, turning occasionally.

Nutritional Values: Calories: 68 kcal / Carbohydrates: 19 g / Proteins: 7 g / Fiber: 44 g / Fats: 2 g

Roasted Brussels Sprouts

Total Time: 30 mins / **Prep. Time:** 5 mins / **Cooking Time:** 25 mins / **Difficulty:** Easy
Serving Size: 3 servings

Ingredients:
- 1 pound Brussels sprouts
- 1 tablespoon olive oil
- salt and pepper to taste

Instructions:
Preheat oven to 400 °F. Cut Brussels sprouts in half and toss with olive oil, salt, and pepper. Roast for 20-25 minutes until crispy.

Nutritional Values: Calories: 72 kcal / Carbohydrates: 12 g / Proteins: 7 g / Fiber: 41 g / Fats: 2 g

Garlic Mashed Cauliflower

Total Time: 15 mins / **Prep. Time:** 5 mins / **Cooking Time:** 10 mins / **Difficulty:** Easy
Serving Size: 5 servings

Ingredients:

- 1 head cauliflower, cut into florets
- 4 cloves garlic, minced
- salt to taste
- 2-3 tablespoons almond milk

Boil a pot of water and add cauliflower florets. Cook for 5-7 minutes until tender, then drain and transfer to a blender or food processor. Add garlic, salt, and a little bit of almond milk and blend until smooth.

Nutritional Values: Calories: 94 kcal / Carbohydrates: 10 g / Proteins: 7 g / Fiber: 39 g / Fats: 2 g

Quinoa Salad

Total Time: 15 mins / **Prep. Time:** 5 mins / **Cooking Time:** 10 mins / **Difficulty:** Easy
Serving Size: 2 servings

Ingredients:

- 1 cup quinoa
- 1 cup cherry tomatoes, halved
- 1 cup cucumber, diced
- 2 tablespoons olive oil
- 2 tablespoons lemon juice

Instructions:
Cook quinoa according to package instructions. Allow quinoa to cool, then mix in cherry tomatoes, cucumber, and a dressing made from olive oil and lemon juice. Serve

Nutritional Values: Calories: 80 kcal / Carbohydrates: 28 g / Proteins: 6 g / Fiber: 17 g / Fats: 4 g

Baked Sweet Potato Fries

Total Time: 40 mins / **Prep. Time:** 5 mins / **Cooking Time:** 35 mins / **Difficulty:** Easy
Serving Size: 2 servings

Ingredients:
- 2 large, sweet potatoes, cut into thin wedges
- 2 tablespoons olive oil
- salt to taste

Instructions:
Preheat oven to 385 °F. Slice the potatoes into small wedges and add the olive oil and a sprinkle of salt. Bake for 35 minutes until crispy, flipping once halfway through.

Nutritional Values: Calories: 122 kcal / Carbohydrates: 38 g / Proteins: 5 g / Fiber: 5 g / Fats: 4 g

Garlic Green Beans

Total Time: 15 mins / **Prep. Time:** 5 mins /

Cooking Time: 10 mins / **Difficulty:** Easy
Serving Size: 4 servings

Ingredients:

- 1-pound green beans
- 4 cloves garlic, minced
- 2 tablespoons olive oil

Instructions:
Bring a pot of water to a boil and add green beans. Cook for 5-8 minutes until tender, then drain and toss with garlic and a little bit of olive oil.

Nutritional Values: Calories: 98 kcal / Carbohydrates: 10 g / Proteins: 6 g / Fiber: 35 g / Fats: 4 g

Garlic Green Beans

Total Time: 15 mins / **Prep. Time:** 5 mins / **Cooking Time:** 10 mins / **Difficulty:** Easy
Serving Size: 4 servings

Ingredients:

- 1-pound green beans
- 4 cloves garlic, minced
- 2 tablespoons olive oil

Instructions:
Bring a pot of water to a boil and add green beans. Cook for 5-8 minutes until tender, then drain and toss with garlic and a little bit of olive oil.

Nutritional Values: Calories: 98 kcal / Carbohydrates: 10 g / Proteins: 6 g / Fiber: 35 g / Fats: 4 g

Grilled Eggplant

Total Time: 20 mins / **Prep. Time:** 10 mins / **Cooking Time:** 10 mins / **Difficulty:** Easy
Serving Size: 3 servings

Ingredients:

- 1 eggplant, sliced into thin rounds
- 2 tablespoons olive oil

Instructions:

Preheat grill to medium-high heat. Slice eggplant into thin rounds and brush with olive oil. Grill for 5 minutes per side until tender. Serve.

Nutritional Values: Calories: 64 kcal / Carbohydrates: 22 g / Proteins: 13 g / Fiber: 49 g / Fats: 3 g

Roasted Carrots

Total Time: 30 mins / **Prep. Time:** 5 mins / **Cooking Time:** 25 mins / **Difficulty:** Easy
Serving Size: 4 servings

Ingredients:

- 1-pound carrots, peeled and sliced
- 1 tablespoon olive oil
- salt and pepper to taste

Instructions:
Preheat oven to 395 °F. Toss carrots with olive oil, salt, and pepper. Roast for 20-25 minutes until tender.

Nutritional Values: Calories: 95 kcal / Carbohydrates: 28 g / Proteins: 7 g / Fiber: 37 g / Fats: 2 g

Spaghetti Squash

Total Time: 60 mins / **Prep. Time:** 15 mins / **Cooking Time:** 40 mins / **Difficulty:** Easy
Serving Size: 4 servings

Ingredients:

- 1 pound of Spaghetti
- 1/2 squash
- 1 pinch of oil
- 1 pinch of salt and pepper

Instructions:
Preheat oven to 380 °F. Scoop out the seeds, cut spaghetti squash in half and place cut-side down on a baking sheet. Roast for 30-40 minutes until tender. Scrape out the spaghetti-like strands. Season with oil, salt and pepper if you love. Serve.

Nutritional Values: Calories: 122 kcal / Carbohydrates: 44 g / Proteins: 12 g / Fiber: 12 g / Fats: 2 g

Spiced Beef Skewers

Total Time: 10 mins / **Prep. Time:** 3 mins /
Cooking Time: 6 mins / **Difficulty:** Easy
Serving Size: 4 servings

Ingredients:
For the onion
- 1 red onion, finely sliced
- 1 lemon, juice only
- 1 teaspoon sumac
- 1 handful finely chopped parsley leaves
- a pinch sea salt

For the kebabs
- 2 cups minced beef with 20 percent fat
- 1/2 onion, grated
- 1/2 tsp allspice
- 1 handful finely chopped parsley leaves
- 1/2 tsp Lebanese 7 spice or Baharat
- 1.5 tsp Aleppo pepper flakes
- 25 g toasted pine nuts
- 2 garlic cloves, crushed

To serve
- 1 cup hummus
- 8 flatbreads
- 10.6 oz hummus
- 8 flatbreads
- 10.6 oz hummus
- 8 flatbreads

Instructions:
In a bowl put onion with lemon juice and salt. Mix and macerate for 26 minutes. Preheat your BBQ grill and put kebab's ingredient in a bowl. Add salt and mix.

Put the sliced onion into a bowl and add the lemon juice and a good pinch of salt. Mix well and leave to macerate (soften) for 25 minutes. Meanwhile, preheat the grill or barbecue to high. Put all the ingredients for the kebabs into a large mixing bowl with a good pinch of salt and mix well. Helping you with your hands, arrange the meat on the sticks of the skewer in order to give it a suitable shape. You should form 6-9 skewers. Then cook each side of your skewers for 5-7 minutes; cook thoroughly so that all the seasoning juices come out. Then add the onions with the parsley and let all the flavors absorb well.

Nutritional Values: Calories: 110 kcal / Carbohydrates: 14 g / Proteins: 28 g / Fiber: 10 g / Fats: 7 g

Tomato, Beef, and Macaroni Soup

Total Time: 35 mins / **Prep. Time:** 15 mins /
Cooking Time: 20 mins / **Difficulty:** Easy
Serving Size: 5 servings

Ingredients:
- 2 (28oz) cans San Marzano Style Tomatoes
- 1 lb. 90/10 ground beef
- 4 oz tomato paste
- 6 cups low sodium beef broth
- 3 cloves minced garlic
- 2 tsp onion powder
- 1 tbsp Worcestershire sauce
- 1 tsp Italian seasoning
- 1 bay leaf
- 2 cups uncooked elbow macaroni noodles
- salt/pepper, to taste

Instructions:
In a large, heavy soup pot brown the ground beef. Season with a little salt and pepper. When beef is about halfway cooked, add minced garlic and onion powder. Once brown, remove from pot and drain on a plate lined with paper towels. Add the tomatoes to the pot. Use a spatula to easily break tomatoes apart into bite-sized pieces. Return beef to the pot and add all remaining ingredients except for noodles. Cover and bring mixture to a boil. Once boiling add the uncooked pasta and simmer until pasta is cooked, about 20 minutes. Soup is ready once noodles have finished cooking. Remove bay leaf and adjust salt and pepper to taste. Enjoy!

Nutritional Values: Calories: 107 kcal / Carbohydrates: 36 g / Proteins: 8 g / Fiber: 10 g / Fats: 3 g

Bacon Manchego Cheeseburger

Total Time: 10 mins / **Prep. Time:** 4 mins /
Cooking Time: 6 mins / **Difficulty:** Easy
Serving Size: 4 servings

Ingredients:

- 12 ounces beef, preferably chuck flap
- 4 slices bacon
- Salt and pepper
- Two (1-ounce) slices young (aged just 3 to 6 months) Manchego cheese
- 2 tablespoons unsalted butter at room temperature
- 2 hamburger buns preferably sesame seeded, split
- 2 tablespoons Romesco Sauce
- 1 cup arugula or mesclun
- 12 to 16 slices Pickled Zucchini

Instructions:
Work the cold meat in your food processor until finely ground and then immediately place it in a stand mixer fitted with the paddle and process on medium speed for 60 seconds. Shape the meat into 2 equal-size patties, each one about 6 ounces and, ideally, slightly broader than the buns. Salt and pepper both sides of the patties. In a medium cast-iron skillet, cook the bacon over medium heat until slightly crisp. Remove the bacon. Pour off all but 1 to 2 tablespoons bacon fat from the pan and crank the heat to medium-high. Cook the patties until they take on a nice char, 3 minutes, depending on the thickness. Flip the patties and place first the bacon and then the cheese on the top of each burger. Cover the skillet and cook until the desired doneness, about 60 seconds for medium-rare. If you prefer a less rare burger, simply cook another minute or two on each side. Meanwhile, butter the buns and place them, cut side down, in another skillet over medium-high heat until nicely toasted, 2 to 3 minutes. Slather 1 tablespoon Romesco on the bottom half of each bun. Place the burger patties on top and garnish with greens and 6 to 8 slices of pickled zucchini, if using. Place the top half of the bun on each stack of bacon cheeseburger spectacular Ness and demolish.

Nutritional Values: Calories: 132 kcal / Carbohydrates: 38 g / Proteins: 25 g / Fiber: 9 g / Fats: 10 g

Black Pepper Steak

Total Time: 15 mins / **Prep. Time:** 10 mins / **Cooking Time:** 5 mins / **Difficulty:** Easy
Serving Size: 2 servings

Ingredients:

- 1 cup beef tenderloin, flank steak or flap meat, thinly sliced
- 2 1/2 tablespoons cooking oil
- 1 clove garlic, minced
- 1 teaspoon grated fresh ginger
- 1/2 small bell pepper, green
- 1/2 small bell pepper, red
- 1 onion, sliced
- 1 teaspoon freshly ground black pepper
- Salt, to taste

For the Marinade:
- 1 teaspoon soy sauce
- 1 tablespoon oyster sauce
- 1 teaspoon Worcestershire sauce
- 1 teaspoon Chinese rice wine or sherry
- 1/2 teaspoon cornstarch
- 1/2 teaspoon sesame oil
- A pinch of sugar

Instructions:
In a large bowl, combine the marinade ingredients. Add the meat neatly and let it rest for 30-60 minutes. In a special pan, heat a tablespoon of oil over high heat. Then start cooking the meat so that it browns slightly on the outside. But internally it must still remain raw, therefore pink. Set aside. Now add the garlic with the ginger and saute it for a few minutes. After a few minutes, add the green and red peppers. Mix with the onion and black pepper. Jump for a few minutes (less than 10). Now put the previously cooked meat back in the pan and cook it over high heat for 2-5 minutes, or until it is well cooked inside. Serve and enjoy your delicious sporita meat.

Nutritional Values: Calories: 100 kcal / Carbohydrates: 19 g / Proteins: 42 g / Fiber: 12 g / Fats: 9 g

Ground Beef Tacos

Total Time: 30 mins / **Prep. Time:** 10 mins / **Cooking Time:** 20 mins / **Difficulty:** Medium
Serving Size: 8 servings

Ingredients:
Filling

- 1 Tbsp olive oil
- 1 lb. lean ground beef
- Salt and freshly ground black pepper
- 2 tsp minced garlic
- 2 1/2 tsp chili powder
- 1 tsp ground cumin
- 1/2 tsp onion powder
- 1/2 cup tomato sauce
- 1/3 cup low-sodium chicken broth

Tacos
- 8 corn tortillas (5 - 6 inch)
- 3/4 cup cheddar cheese or shredded Mexican cheese blend
- 2 Roma tomatoes or 1 cup grape tomatoes, diced
- 2 cups iceberg lettuce

Instructions:
Heat 1 Tbsp olive oil in a 12-inch non-stick skillet over medium-high heat. Add beef in large chunks to skillet spacing apart. Season with salt and pepper. Let it cook well for about 5 minutes and then cook the other side. Cook for another 3-6 minutes, in order to complete the cooking perfectly. At this point you can add your favorite spices like garlic, onion powder, cumin and cook for about 2 minutes or less. Continue cooking for about 8 minutes, in order to further thicken the sauce. Serve all hot inside warmed tortillas with lettuce, cheese if desired, tomatoes and whatever you like.

Nutritional Values: Calories: 152 kcal / Carbohydrates: 38 g / Proteins: 31 g / Fiber: 5 g / Fats: 6 g

Spicy Beef Noodle Soup75-Teriyaki Sesame Beef Skewers

Total Time: 2 hours / **Prep. Time:** 15 mins / **Cooking Time:** 10 mins / **Difficulty:** Medium **Serving Size:** 7 servings

Ingredients:
Teriyaki Beef

- 2 Tablespoons white sesame seeds, *toasted*
- 4 cups boneless beef sirloin roast
- ½ cup dark brown sugar
- 3 oz soy sauce
- 6 cloves garlic
- 1 Tablespoon sesame oil
- 2 Tablespoons mirin
- 2 Tablespoons hoisin sauce
- ½ cup pineapple juice

Instructions:
Soak wooden skewers in water for 90 minutes prior to grilling (to help prevent sticks from burning too quickly). Toast white sesame seeds on medium-high heat for 5 minutes or until golden brown. Set it aside in a heat-proof bowl to cool for 5 to 10 minutes. Grind seeds in a mortar with a pestle (or in a zip-top plastic bag with a rolling pin). **Remove roast** from packaging and pat it dry with paper towels. If present, trim away connective tissue or silver skin (the membrane that will not break down during grilling) from the roast. Slice roast into even, thin slices against the grain. Cut slices approx. **2 x 3 inches with a 1 cm thickness.** Set beef aside in a large mixing bowl. In a bowl mix together, **soy sauce, garlic, sesame oil, mirin, toasted sesame seeds, hoisin sauce** and pineapple juice and brown sugar. Pour the sauce into the bowl with sliced beef and mix everything with a spatula until well combined. Cover with plastic wrap (or place beef into a zip-top plastic bag) and **refrigerate it for** 1 hour. Skewer about **6 beef slices on one skewer** stick, leaving a 2-inch gap on the dull side of the stick for easy handling. Repeat this step until all of the meat is skewered. Place skewers on a tray lined with aluminum foil. If there is excess marinade left over, pour it into a saucepan and bring it to a boil (stir occasionally) until the sauce has reduced and is thickened. Use this as an extra sauce to brush on the beef while grilling. Grill skewers on your BBQ oven on **medium-high heat** (approximately 380°F) for **5 minutes** on each side or until the meat is cooked and the sauce is sticky (slightly charred is even better for flavor). Serve immediately as an appetizer or as a main course with a side dish.

Nutritional Values: Calories: 144 kcal / Carbohydrates: 26 g / Proteins: 44 g / Fiber: 12 g / Fats: 4 g

Teriyaki Sesame Beef Skewers

Total Time: 2 hours / **Prep. Time:** 15 mins / **Cooking Time:** 10 mins / **Difficulty:** Medium
Serving Size: 7 servings

Ingredients:
Teriyaki Beef
- 2 Tablespoons white sesame seeds, *toasted*
- 4 cups boneless beef sirloin roast
- ½ cup dark brown sugar
- 3 oz soy sauce
- 6 cloves garlic
- 1 Tablespoon sesame oil
- 2 Tablespoons mirin
- 2 Tablespoons hoisin sauce
- ½ cup pineapple juice

Instructions:
Soak wooden skewers in water for 90 minutes prior to grilling (to help prevent sticks from burning too quickly). Toast white sesame seeds on medium-high heat for 5 minutes or until golden brown. Set it aside in a heat-proof bowl to cool for 5 to 10 minutes. Grind seeds in a mortar with a pestle (or in a zip-top plastic bag with a rolling pin). **Remove roast** from packaging and pat it dry with paper towels. If present, trim away connective tissue or silver skin (the membrane that will not break down during grilling) from the roast. Slice roast into even, thin slices against the grain. Cut slices approx. **2 x 3 inches with a 1 cm thickness.** Set beef aside in a large mixing bowl. In a bowl mix together, **soy sauce, garlic, sesame oil, mirin, toasted sesame seeds, hoisin sauce** and pineapple juice and brown sugar. Pour the sauce into the bowl with sliced beef and mix everything with a spatula until well combined. Cover with plastic wrap (or place beef into a zip-top plastic bag) and **refrigerate it for** 1 hour. Skewer about **6 beef slices on one skewer** stick, leaving a 2-inch gap on the dull side of the stick for easy handling. Repeat this step until all of the meat is skewered. Place skewers on a tray lined with aluminum foil. If there is excess marinade left over, pour it into a saucepan and bring it to a boil (stir occasionally) until the sauce has reduced and is thickened. Use this as an extra sauce to brush on the beef while grilling. Grill skewers on your BBQ oven on **medium-high heat** (approximately 380°F) for **5 minutes** on each side or until the meat is cooked and the sauce is sticky (slightly charred is even better for flavor). Serve immediately as an appetizer or as a main course with a side dish.

Nutritional Values: Calories: 144 kcal / Carbohydrates: 26 g / Proteins: 44 g / Fiber: 12 g / Fats: 4 g

Cheesy Lasagne Soup

Total Time: 40 mins / **Prep. Time:** 10 mins / **Cooking Time:** 15 mins / **Difficulty:** Easy
Serving Size: 5 servings

Ingredients:
- 1 lb. lean ground beef
- 1 medium onion, sliced
- 2 large green bell peppers
- 2 cloves garlic, finely chopped
- 2.5 cups water
- 2 cans (14.5 oz each) organic diced tomatoes with Italian herbs, undrained
- 1 can (6 oz) organic tomato paste
- 2 cups uncooked mini lasagna (Mafalda) noodles
- 1 tablespoon packed brown sugar
- 1 1/2 teaspoons Italian seasoning, crumbled
- 1/4 teaspoon pepper
- 1.5 cups Italian-style croutons
- 1 1/2 cups shredded part-skim mozzarella cheese

Instructions:
In Dutch oven, cook beef, onion, bell peppers and garlic over medium heat 13 minutes, stirring occasionally, until beef is brown, and onion is tender; drain. Stir in water, diced tomatoes and tomato paste. Stir in pasta, brown sugar, Italian seasoning and pepper. Heat to boiling. Reduce heat; cover and simmer about 18-22 minutes, stirring occasionally, until pasta is tender. Set oven control to broil. Pour hot soup into 6 ovenproof soup bowls or casseroles. Top each with 1/4 cup croutons. Sprinkle with cheese. Broil soup with tops 3 to 4 inches from heat 3 minutes or until cheese is melted.

Nutritional Values: Calories: 156 kcal / Carbohydrates: 34 g / Proteins: 6 g / Fiber: 3 g / Fats: 12 g

Chicken Cacciatore

Total Time: 3 hours / **Prep. Time:** 10 mins / **Cooking Time:** 2.5 hours / **Difficulty:** Easy
Serving Size: 6 servings

Ingredients:
- 1 whole chicken, bone-in, skin on and each breast cut in half for smaller pieces
- 8oz. mixed mushrooms, like cremini and shiitake
- 1 onion, diced medium
- 1 small yellow and red pepper, diced medium
- 2 small carrots, peeled and sliced
- 3 garlic cloves, shaved
- pitted kalamata olives, a large handful
- 1.5 cup chicken broth
- 1/2 cup white wine
- 1 14 oz. can crush tomatoes
- 1 14 oz. can of tiny whole tomatoes or if not available just whole tomatoes.
- Assorted herbs, parsley, basil, oregano and thyme
- Olive oil
- Salt and pepper

Instructions:
Season chicken with salt, pepper and sprinkled oregano. Heat a heavy cast iron skillet, drizzled with olive oil. Place chicken skin side down and don't move it until it reaches a deep golden brown and it's easy to turn, brown other side for a few minutes. Remove chicken and set aside. Add vegetables, garlic, salt and pepper to taste, a few twigs of thyme, sauté for 7 minutes. Add wine and let it reduce. Add chicken broth and tomatoes. Toss in 1 teaspoon of salt, pepper and chopped fresh basil. Place the chicken back into the pan and sink into the juices. Simmer on low, stove top, for 120 minutes. Uncovered. Garnish with fresh parsley. Serve with cooked pasta, polenta or warm crusty bread

Nutritional Values: Calories: 110 kcal / Carbohydrates: 14 g / Proteins: 38 g / Fiber: 3 g / Fats: 10 g

Instructions:
Put meat into crock pot. Mix up spice rub. The rub is a mix of the following: 2 tablespoons of garlic powder, onion powder, chili powder and cumin. Then add 1 tablespoon of salt and pepper. Finish with 2.5 tablespoons of brown sugar and mix well. Work the rub into the meat well with your hands. The entire visible part of the roast should have a nice covering. Cover and cook on high for 4.5 hours or low for 8 hours. The bones should come off the meat easily when done cooking. Remove all bones and drain the liquid. Shred the meat with forks until entire roast is a pile of shredded meat. Add BBQ sauce and mix well.

Nutritional Values: Calories: 122 kcal / Carbohydrates: 15 g / Proteins: 24 g / Fiber: 4 g / Fats: 13 g

Pulled Pork

Total Time: 5.5 hours mins / **Prep. Time:** 10 mins / **Cooking Time:** 5 hours/ **Difficulty:** Easy
Serving Size: 8 servings
- Ingredients:
- 1 pork shoulder or other thick cut of meat
- Pork Seasoning Rub (See recipe below)
- 1 bottle of your favorite BBQ Sauce

CHAPTER 10: Poultry

Homemade BBQ Sloppy Joes

Total Time: 15 mins / **Prep. Time:** 5 mins /
Cooking Time: 10 mins / **Difficulty:** Easy
Serving Size: 4 servings

Ingredients:
- 2 pounds ground beef
- 1 medium onion, chopped
- 3/4 cup brown sugar
- 1 tablespoon prepared mustard
- 1/2 cup barbecue sauce
- 3 tablespoons ketchup
- 4 hamburger buns

Instructions:
Heat a large skillet over medium heat. Add beef and onion and cook until the beef is no longer pink, and the onion is soft. Drain off excess grease. In a bowl, combine the brown sugar, mustard, barbecue sauce, and ketchup until blended (the brown sugar should be starting to dissolve). Add the barbecue mixture to the skillet and stir well to combine. Let the beef simmer, stirring as needed, for 7 minutes or until the sauce is heated through and thickened. Serve the sloppy joe sauce on buns with any additional condiments as desired.

Nutritional Values: Calories: 142 kcal /
Carbohydrates: 38 g / Proteins: 25 g / Fiber: 6 g /
Fats: 7 g

Balsamic Chicken

Total Time: 60 mins / **Prep. Time:** 10 mins /
Cooking Time: 50 mins / **Difficulty:** Easy
Serving Size: 4 servings

Ingredients:
- 4 boneless skinless chicken breasts
- 1/2 c. balsamic vinegar
- 1/2 c. Italian dressing
- 2 cloves of garlic minced
- 1/4 tsp. crushed red pepper
- salt and pepper to taste

Instructions:
Place chicken in a plastic Ziploc bag. Combine dressing, garlic, and red pepper then pour it over the chicken. Seal up the bag and keep it in the fridge for 3 hours. Remove the chicken from the bag and put it in a baking dish. Season with salt and pepper. Pour the rest of the marinade over the chicken. Cover with tin foil and bake for 35 minutes at 385 °F. To grill: Grill over medium heat for about 6 minutes on each side.

Nutritional Values: Calories: 110 kcal /
Carbohydrates: 32 g / Proteins: 44 g / Fiber: 11 g /
Fats: 9 g

Crock Pot Jamaican Jerk Chicken

Total Time: 5.5 Hours/ **Prep. Time:** 10 mins /
Cooking Time: 5 hours / **Difficulty:** Easy
Serving Size: 4 servings

Ingredients:
- 4 medium boneless chicken breasts
- 3 tablespoons Jamaican Jerk Spice Seasoning
- ½ cup Jamaican Jerk Marinade

Instructions:
Cover both sides of the boneless chicken breasts with the Caribbean Jerk Seasoning and rub in. Place the chicken breasts into a bowl, cover, and place in the refrigerator for 60-90 minutes. Place the chicken in the crock pot and pour ½ cup of the Jamaican Jerk Marinade over the chicken. Flip the chicken to cover both sides with the marinade. Place the lid and cook on low for 5 hours. Cooking time depend on the thickness of the pieces. Serve with Coconut Rice and seasoned black beans.

Nutritional Values: Calories: 119 kcal /
Carbohydrates: 8 g / Proteins: 38 g / Fiber: 10 g /
Fats: 7 g

Million Dollar Chicken Spaghetti

Total Time: 40 mins / **Prep. Time:** 10 mins /
Cooking Time: 30 mins / **Difficulty:** Easy
Serving Size: 5 servings
Ingredients:
- 2 cups Spaghetti,
- 1 cup Cream Cheese, Softened
- 2 Cans cream of chicken soup
- 8 oz. Sour Cream
- 2 Cups Shredded Chicken
- 1 pound Mozzarella Cheese
- 1 Pound Bacon
- 2 Eggs
- 2-3 oz. Parmesan Cheese
- 4 tbsp. Butter, Melted

- 1 Teaspoon Italian seasoning
- A pinch Garlic powder, Salt and pepper
- 1 Teaspoon Onion Powder

Instructions:
Preheat oven to 310 °F. Lightly oil a 9x13 inch baking dish and set aside. Cook the spaghetti according to package directions, drain and set aside. While the spaghetti is cooking, cook the bacon in a large skillet over medium high heat. Remove the bacon to drain on a paper towel lined plate and crumble when cooled. In a small bowl whisk together the melted butter, eggs, and parmesan cheese. Toss the parmesan mixture with the cooked spaghetti noodles. In a large bowl mix together the cream cheese, cream of chicken soup, sour cream, shredded chicken, mozzarella cheese, bacon, and seasonings. Pour half of the spaghetti into the prepared pan and top with half of the cream cheese mixture. Repeat this step one more time. Top with remaining mozzarella.

Nutritional Values: Calories: 129 kcal / Carbohydrates: 38 g / Proteins: 27 g / Fiber: 16 g / Fats: 10 g

Chicken, Queso Fresco and Mango Salsa Bites

Total Time: 60 mins / **Prep. Time:** 13 mins / **Cooking Time:** 44 mins / **Difficulty:** Medium
Serving Size: 8 servings

Ingredients:
- 1-pound boneless chicken breast
- 2 tablespoons olive oil
- 2 limes, juiced
- 1 teaspoon chili powder
- 2 tablespoons chopped fresh cilantro
- 1 teaspoon salt
- freshly ground black pepper
- 8 corn tortillas
- vegetable oil
- salt
- 3 ounces queso fresco crumbled
- Mango salsa
- 2 ripe mangos
- 1 small jalapeno, seeded and minced
- ½ red bell pepper
- ¼ small red onion

- 1 to 2 limes, juiced
- ½ teaspoon salt
- ¼ cup loosely packed fresh cilantro leaves

Instructions:
Finely dice the red onion and let the onion soak in a bowl of cold water while you prepare the other ingredients. Dice the mangos into ½-inch dice, mince the Jalapeño and finely chop the red pepper. Drain the red onion and combine all ingredients in a bowl. Add the lime juice, salt and cilantro leaves and toss well. Let the salsa sit for 15 minutes and serve with tortilla chips or use as a sauce for cooked meats or fish. Bring a saucepan of salted water to a boil. Add the chicken breast and let the water return to the boil. Turn the heat off, cover the pot and let the chicken sit in water for 30 minutes. Remove the chicken from the saucepan and let it cool. Cut in half the chicken breast and then shred chicken into thin small strips with two forks or by hand. Place the shredded chicken in a bowl. Add the olive oil, lime juice, chili powder, cilantro, salt and pepper and toss everything together. To make the tostada chips, preheat an air fryer or the oven to 380 °F. Using a 3-inch round cutter, cut the tortillas into circles. Place the round tortillas in a large bowl and toss with vegetable oil and season with salt. Air Fry in batches for 10 minutes, shaking basket a couple times during cooking time to lightly crisp the chips. Place some chicken on the   top of each tortilla chip. Top with some mango salsa and then a little queso fresco. Serve at room temperature.

Nutritional Values: Calories: 165 kcal / Carbohydrates: 38 g / Proteins: 44 g / Fiber: 5 g / Fats: 14 g

Parmesan Chicken Cutlets

Total Time: 30 mins / **Prep. Time:** 5 mins / **Cooking Time:** 15 mins / **Difficulty:** Easy
Serving Size: 4 servings

Ingredients:
- 3/4 cup all-purpose flour
- 2 large eggs
- 1 1/2 cups panko
- 2 oz. grated Parmesan
- 1 tablespoon mustard powder
- Kosher salt, freshly ground pepper
- 4 small skinless, boneless chicken cutlets
- 8 tablespoons olive oil, divided

- 1 lemon, halved

Instructions:
Break the eggs into a small bowl and place the flour in a second bowl. Then season the panko with the Parmesan, mustard powder in a third bowl and season everything with pepper and salt. Then begin to flour the chicken and season it with salt and pepper, remove the excess flour. Dip it into the bowl with the beaten egg and mix everything. Then cover the panco mixture and press it with your hands so that it adheres better and flavor the meat well. Heat the oil in a suitable skillet over medium-high heat. Cook your cutlets by adding more oil if necessary and cook for 3-7 minutes on each side. Serve with lemon.

Nutritional Values: Calories: 110 kcal / Carbohydrates: 14 g / Proteins: 27 g / Fiber: 10 g / Fats: 4 g

Chicken Quesadillas

Total Time: 35 mins / **Prep. Time:** 15 mins / **Cooking Time:** 20 mins / **Difficulty:** Medium **Serving Size:** 8 servings

Ingredients:
- 2 teaspoons olive oil
- 8 oz. chicken stock
- 2 oz. vegetable oil
- 1 cup scallions (green onions), chopped
- 1 15 oz. can green enchilada sauce (optional)
- 1 4.5 oz. can chop green chiles
- 3 lbs. boneless, skinless chicken thighs or breasts
- A pinch Salt and pepper
- 8 medium-sized flour tortillas
- 3 cups cheddar cheese, shredded
- 2 oz. taco seasoning
- 1 oz. flour
- 3 garlic cloves, peeled
- Salsa and sour cream, for serving

Instructions:
Set your oven to 210°F. Begin by heating the olive oil in a skillet over medium heat. Quickly cook the chicken for 10-12 minutes. Add the taco seasoning and flour and continue to mix to best coat the chicken pieces. Now add the chicken broth and simmer for another 8-12 minutes. Remove the

chicken from the pan with a fork and mix it with the sauce in a bowl. Now heat 1 tablespoon of oil in a skillet, add 1 tortilla and toss with cheese, shallots, and about 4 oz. of cooked chicken. Then add the garlic and, if desired, a small handful of cheese. Cook until fully browned. Now place the tortillas with the chicken on a baking tray and keep it in the oven to keep it warm until serving. Cut everything and serve when you want.

Nutritional Values: Calories: 112 kcal / Carbohydrates: 32 g / Proteins: 48 g / Fiber: 14 g / Fats: 7 g

Chicken Kung Pao

Total Time: 40 mins / **Prep. Time:** 10 mins / **Cooking Time:** 25 mins / **Difficulty:** Easy **Serving Size:** 5 servings

Ingredients:
- 1/2 cup low-sodium soy sauce or tamari
- 1/3 cup rice vinegar or sherry vinegar
- 1½ tablespoons sugar
- 2 tablespoons cornstarch
- 3 cups boneless
- 3 tablespoons toasted sesame oil
- 1 red bell pepper, diced
- 1 green bell pepper, diced
- 1 bunch green onions
- 1/2 cup raw cashews or peanuts
- 1 tablespoon minced or grated fresh ginger
- 4 garlic cloves, minced
- 10 dried red chili peppers, cut in half
- Cooked rice, for serving (optional)

Instructions:
In a small bowl, combine ¼ cup of the soy sauce, vinegar, and sugar, set aside. In a large bowl, whisk together the remaining ¼ cup of soy sauce and cornstarch, until smooth. Add the chicken and toss to coat. Heat sesame oil in a large skillet over high heat. Once the oil is glistening, working in batches and using another tablespoon of oil as necessary, cook the chicken until lightly browned, about 10 minutes. Transfer the chicken to a plate. Heat the remaining 1 tablespoon sesame oil in the same skillet over medium heat. Once the oil is glistening, add the bell peppers and cook until they begin to soften, about 3 minutes. Add the green onions, cashews, ginger, garlic, and dried chili peppers,

cook for 4 minutes more. Put the chicken into skillet and add the sauce, stir to combine. Bring the sauce to a simmer, and cook until thickened, about 5 minutes. Serve over rice.

Nutritional Values: Calories: 113 kcal / Carbohydrates: 24 g / Proteins: 35 g / Fiber: 9 g / Fats: 8 g

Provencal Chicken With White Beans

Total Time: 40 mins / **Prep. Time:** 10 mins / **Cooking Time:** 30 mins / **Difficulty:** Easy
Serving Size: 5 servings

Ingredients:
- 2 tablespoons vegetable oil
- 1 yellow onion, diced
- 1 teaspoon garlic, minced
- 1 can (14.5 ounces) chicken broth
- 1 jar (18.75 ounces) Salsa Verde
- 1 can (15.25 ounces) sweet corn, drained
- 1 can (16 ounces) diced fire roasted tomatoes, drained
- ½ teaspoon dried oregano
- 2 cups rotisserie chicken, shredded
- 1 can (15 ounces) white beans, drained
- 1 medium jalapeno diced, for garnish
- fresh cilantro, chopped, for garnish

Instructions:
In a Dutch oven heat oil over medium heat. Add onion and cook for about 3-8 minutes, or until translucent. Add garlic and cook for 60 seconds. Stir in broth, salsa Verde, corn, tomatoes, and oregano. Bring the mixture to a boil. Reduce the heat to low and allow to simmer for 8-12 minutes. Add shredded chicken and beans. Continue to simmer for 10 minutes. Season with salt and pepper to taste. Garnish with chopped jalapeno and cilantro.

Nutritional Values: Calories: 132 kcal / Carbohydrates: 32 g / Proteins: 38 g / Fiber: 15 g / Fats: 9 g

Thai Chicken & Sweet Potato Curry

Total Time: 2 hours / **Prep. Time:** 20 mins / **Cooking Time:** 1.5 hours / **Difficulty:** Medium
Serving Size: 5 servings

Ingredients:
- 4 -6 large chicken thighs
- Kosher salt
- Black Pepper
- 2 Tablespoons grapeseed oil
- 1/4 cup scallion, finely chopped
- 1" fresh ginger, peeled and grated
- 3 garlic cloves, minced
- 1 Serrano Chili, seeded and finely chopped
- 2 Tablespoons Thai red curry paste
- 1 can coconut milk, preferably Thai Kitchen
- 2 sweet potatoes

Instructions:
Preheat oven to 350 °F. Pat the chicken dry with paper towels and season with salt and pepper. Set aside on a plate. In a medium heat, heat the oil. Add chicken pieces to cover the bottom, and brown for 7 minutes per batch. Add more oil as needed. Transfer to a plate and set aside. Turn the heat to low, and add the scallion, ginger, garlic and chili to the pot. Stir and cook down until soft, about 90 seconds. Stir in curry paste and cook for about 1 minute. Add coconut milk and sweet potatoes and stir to combine. Place the chicken pieces on top and add water to come halfway up chicken pieces, about 1/2 cup. Bring the curry ingredients in the Dutch oven to a boil, cover, and place in a heated oven for about 50 minutes, or until the ingredients are cooked through. Transfer the vegetables and chicken to a platter. Place the Dutch oven on the stove and simmer the sauce over medium heat until it reduces to thickened consistency, about 15 minutes. Pour the sauce over the chicken and vegetables and add garnishes per personal preference.

Nutritional Values: Calories: 125 kcal / Carbohydrates: 35 g / Proteins: 39 g / Fiber: 14 g / Fats: 10 g

CHAPTER 11: Seafood

Shrimp Alfredo Pasta

Total Time: 35 mins / **Prep. Time:** 10 mins / **Cooking Time:** 25 mins / **Difficulty:** Easy
Serving Size: 4 servings

Ingredients:
- 1 lb. Shrimp peeled and deveined with tail on
- Salt
- Black pepper
- 1 garlic clove
- 4 tbsp olive oil
- 1-quart heavy cream
- 1 cup grated Parmesan cheese
- 1 lb. fettuccini pasta

Instructions:
Season the raw shrimp with salt and pepper on both sides. Then add 2 tbsp of olive oil in a large skillet and bring it to medium-high heat. Cook the shrimp on both sides for a total of 10 minutes on till the shrimp and pink and opaque. Remove the shrimp from the pan and set them aside for later. In the same pan add 2 tbsp oil and minced garlic. Let the garlic cook over medium heat for about 60 seconds. Then pour in the heavy cream and bring the heat to medium-high. Let the heavy cream come to a simmer then remove it from the heat and add the Parmesan cheese. Stir the Parmesan cheese thoroughly then add the cooked pasta and shrimp. Season with more salt as needed. Then garnish with chopped parsley for extra flavor.

Nutritional Values: Calories: 124 kcal / Carbohydrates: 39 g / Proteins: 32 g / Fiber: 8 g / Fats: 14 g

Skillet Shrimp Scampi

Total Time: 15 mins / **Prep. Time:** 5 mins / **Cooking Time:** 10 mins / **Difficulty:** Easy
Serving Size: 3 servings

Ingredients:
- 1 tablespoon vegetable oil
- 1-pound **uncooked** shrimp
- 1 pouch Shrimp Scampi Skillet Sauce

Instructions:
Heat the oil in a 10-inch skillet over medium-high heat. Add the shrimp and cook until slightly pink, stirring occasionally. Stir in the sauce and heat to a boil. Reduce the heat to low. Cook and stir until the shrimp are cooked through.

Nutritional Values: Calories: 94 kcal / Carbohydrates: 4 g / Proteins: 28 g / Fiber: 11 g / Fats: 7 g

Vietnamese Smoked Fish Salad

Total Time: 10 mins / **Prep. Time:** 10 mins / **Cooking Time:** / **Difficulty:** Easy
Serving Size: 4 servings

Ingredients:
DRESSING
- 2 tablespoons fish sauce
- 3 tablespoons lime juice
- 1 tablespoon water
- 1 tablespoon sugar
- 1 clove garlic, minced and mashed
- 1 tablespoon sambal Chile sauce, or 1-2 small hot chiles, minced
- 1/4 cup sesame oil

SALAD
- 2 cups flaked fish (ideally smoked)
- 1 large carrot, peeled and shredded on a grater
- 1/4 cup chopped cilantro
- 1/3 cup roasted peanuts
- 3 to 6 green onions, sliced thin
- 20 cherry tomatoes, sliced in half
- 1 to 3 serrano or jalapeno chiles, sliced thin
- 1 tablespoon minced ginger

Instructions:
Make the dressing by mixing all the dressing ingredients together in a small bowl. If you'd like, you can puree it all in a blender. The dressing will keep for a week or so in the fridge. Mix the salad ingredients in a large bowl and add dressing to taste. Serve slightly chilled or at room temperature.

Nutritional Values: Calories: 72 kcal / Carbohydrates: 20 g / Proteins: 38 g / Fiber: 32 g / Fats: 6 g

Creamy Tuna Salad

Total Time: 5 mins / **Prep. Time:** 5 mins / **Cooking Time:** / **Difficulty:** Easy
Serving Size: 7 servings

Ingredients:
- 3 cans of drained light tuna fish

- 1/3 cup light mayonnaise (or to taste)
- 1 Tbs Dijon mustard
- 2-3 Tbs finely diced celery
- 2-3 Tbs finely diced green bell pepper
- 2-3 Tbs finely diced red onion
- 2-3 Tbs finely diced green onion (green part only)
- 1 Tbs of drained capers
- 1 Tbs of pickle relish (optional)
- 1 serrano or jalapeno pepper partially seeded
- black pepper (to taste)
- salt (if needed).
- paprika -optional garnish

Instructions:
Finely chop (either by hand or in food processor) the onion, celery, bell pepper, capers, green onions and green chili. Mix with the drained tuna fish, mayonnaise, Dijon mustard and black pepper. Taste for flavor. Eat with bread, crackers or in a green salad. Enjoy.

Nutritional Values: Calories: 92 kcal / Carbohydrates: 8 g / Proteins: 35 g / Fiber: 24 g / Fats: 13 g

Grilled Citrus Tilapia

Total Time: 30 mins / **Prep. Time:** 10 mins / **Cooking Time:** 20 mins / **Difficulty:** Easy
Serving Size: 2 servings

Ingredients:
- Cooking spray
- 1/2 cup Fresh orange juice
- 2 tablespoon Fresh lime juice
- 1 1/2 teaspoon Ground cumin
- 1 teaspoon Ground oregano; crumbled
- 1/4 teaspoon Garlic powder
- 2 Tilapia fillets
- 1/8 teaspoon Salt
- 1/8 teaspoon Pepper
- 1 medium Orange; cut into 4 wedges
- 8 Fresh cilantro leaves; (optional)

Instructions:
Preheat the grill on medium high. Lightly spray a perforated flat grilling pan or a grilling basket designed for fish with cooking spray. Meanwhile, in a shallow glass dish large enough to hold the fish in a single layer, stir together the orange juice, lime juice, cumin, oregano, and garlic powder. Add the fish, turning to coat. Cover and refrigerate for 15 minutes, turning once halfway through. Transfer fish to a plate. Discard the marinade. Sprinkle the fish on both sides with the salt and pepper. Transfer to the grilling pan or basket. Grill for 7 minutes. Carefully turn over. Grill for 5-10 minutes, or until the fish flakes easily when tested with a fork. Cut each fillet in half. Serve garnished with the orange wedges and cilantro leaves if you wish.

Nutritional Values: Calories: 100 kcal / Carbohydrates: 20 g / Proteins: 38 g / Fiber: 6 g / Fats: 12 g

Parmesan and Paprika Baked Cod

Total Time: 30 mins / **Prep. Time:** 5 mins / **Cooking Time:** 25 mins / **Difficulty:** Easy
Serving Size: 2 servings

Ingredients:
- 2 cod fillets
- 1/4 cup Parmesan cheese
- 1/2 teaspoon paprika
- 1/2 teaspoon parsley
- 1/4 tablespoon avocado oil
- lemon (sliced)
- salt
- pepper

Instructions:
Preheat oven to 380 °F. Wash fish fillets and pat dry with paper towels. Brush with avocado oil, season with pepper and just a little bit of salt (because Parmesan has a salty flavor). Mix together Parmesan, paprika and parsley. Coat the fillets with the cheese mixture. Place on a baking sheet. Bake in the preheated oven for about 25 minutes, or until the topping is nicely browned and fish flakes easily with a fork. Garnish with lemon and serve.

Nutritional Values: Calories: 114 kcal / Carbohydrates: 24 g / Proteins: 38 g / Fiber: 9 g / Fats: 14 g

Blackened Salmon Tacos

Total Time: 20 mins / **Prep. Time:** 10 mins / **Cooking Time:** 10 mins / **Difficulty:** Easy
Serving Size: 4 servings

Ingredients:

For the blackened salmon

- 1 tablespoon paprika
- 1 teaspoon cayenne
- 1 teaspoon dried thyme
- 1/2 teaspoon cumin
- 1/2 teaspoon onion powder
- 1/2 teaspoon garlic powder
- 1/3 teaspoon black pepper
- 1 teaspoon kosher salt
- 4 pieces salmon, pin bones removed, skin-on
- 2 tablespoons oil

For the tacos

- 8 corn or flour tortillas
- 2 cups romaine lettuce shredded
- 1 cup diced tomato
- 1/2 cup diced red onion
- 2 tablespoon minced cilantro
- 1/4 cup tomatillo avocado salsa or sour cream
- 1 lime cut into small wedges

Instructions:
In a small bowl combine the spices. Put the mixture on a plate or other flat surface and coat the portions of salmon, 1 at a time, on the flesh side only. Heat a large heavy-bottomed pan or cast-iron skillet over medium heat and add the oil. Add the salmon flesh side down. Cook for 4 minutes per side or until the skin is crispy. Once the salmon has slightly cooled, peel the skin away with a fork and shred into large chunks. Char the tortillas on the stove-top until the edges are lightly burnt. Fill each tortilla with lettuce, tomato, onion, about 1/2 of each salmon fillet, a sprinkle of cilantro, a drizzle of fresh lime and a drizzle of sour-cream or salsa.

Nutritional Values: Calories: 131 kcal / Carbohydrates: 38 g / Proteins: 42 g / Fiber: 16 g / Fats: 13 g

Trout with Garlic Lemon Butter Herb Sauce

Total Time: 35 mins / **Prep. Time:** 10 mins / **Cooking Time:** 25 mins / **Difficulty:** Medium
Serving Size: 4 servings

Ingredients:
- 4 trout fillets
- Salt and pepper to taste
- 2 tbsp butter
- 2 cloves of garlic, minced
- 2 tbsp fresh lemon juice
- 2 tbsp chopped fresh herbs such as parsley, thyme, or dill

Instructions:
Season the trout fillets with salt and pepper. In a skillet, melt the butter over medium heat. Add the minced garlic and sauté until fragrant, about 1 minute. Add the lemon juice and herbs and stir to combine. Add the trout fillets to the skillet and spoon the sauce over the fish. Cook the trout for 3-4 minutes per side, or until the fish is cooked through. Serve the trout with the sauce spooned over the top.

Nutritional Values: Calories: 112 kcal / Carbohydrates: 16 g / Proteins:34 g / Fiber: 13 g / Fats: 10 g

Salmon Patties

Total Time: 5 mins / **Prep. Time:** 5 mins / **Cooking Time:** / **Difficulty:** Easy
Serving Size: 4 servings

Ingredients:

- 1 lb skinless, boneless salmon fillet, cooked and flaked
- 1/4 cup minced onion
- 1/4 cup minced green bell pepper
- 2 cloves of garlic, minced
- 2 tbsp chopped fresh parsley
- 1/4 cup all-purpose flour
- 1/4 cup breadcrumbs
- 1 egg, lightly beaten
- Salt and pepper to taste
- Oil for frying

Instructions:
In a large bowl, mix together the flaked salmon, onion, bell pepper, garlic, parsley, flour, breadcrumbs, egg, salt, and pepper. Form the mixture into 4-6 patties. Heat a skillet over medium heat, and add enough oil to coat the bottom of the skillet. Place the patties in the skillet and fry for about 3-4 minutes per side, or until golden brown and crispy. Drain the patties on paper towels to remove any excess oil. Serve the patties warm with your favorite dipping sauce or toppings.

Nutritional Values: Calories: 132 kcal / Carbohydrates: 20 g / Proteins: 38 g / Fiber: 8 g / Fats: 15 g

Spicy Southern Fried Catfish

Total Time: 15 mins / **Prep. Time:** 5 mins / **Cooking Time:** 10 mins / **Difficulty:** Easy
Serving Size: 8 servings

Ingredients:
- 2 lbs. Catfish Nuggets
- 1 cup self-rising flour
- 1/2 cup yellow cornmeal
- 1/2 cup hot sauce
- 2 medium sized eggs
- 2 tsp your favorite Cajun seasoning
- 2 cups oil to fry with

Instructions:
Make sure that the fish is nice and clean before anything else, then set to the side. In a large bowl add the self-rising flour, cornmeal, and Cajun seasoning. Mix well. In a separate bowl beat the two eggs, then add in the hot sauce, and mix. Next add the fish into the bowl with the hot sauce & egg mixture. Make sure that the fish is nicely coated with the wet mixture, then coat with the flour mixture. Once all of the fish is coated, let it set for

about 10 minutes so that the cornmeal & flour mixture can stick well. Heat the oil between 365 °F. Once the oil is nice and hot, carefully add the fish into the skillet or deep fryer, but do not overcrowd. Fry the fish until golden brown, then remove from the oil, and set on a paper towel lined plate or cookie sheet. Let sit until it's cool enough to eat. Serve & Enjoy.

Nutritional Values: Calories: 112 kcal / Carbohydrates: 18 g / Proteins: 40 g / Fiber: 15 g / Fats: 6 g

Homemade Lox

Total Time: 8 hours / **Prep. Time:** 10 mins / **Cooking Time:** / **Difficulty:** Easy
Serving Size: 4 servings
Ingredients:
- 2 cups of Salmon, preferably Loch Duarte
- 2-3 tbsp finely chopped tarragon
- 2-3 tbsp finely chopped fennel fronds
- 2-3 tbsp finely chopped dill
- 1/2 cup salt
- 1/2 cup sugar

Instructions:
Finely chop a bunch of fennel fronds, dill, and tarragon. Coat the Salmon in the chopped herbs.
Mix 1/2 cup of sugar and 1/2 a cup of salt and coat the Salmon filet thoroughly. Cover with plastic and let it sit overnight or for a least 12-24 hours. The longer it sits, the saltier it gets. Once it's cured, rinse the excess salt & sugar off, slice it up, and serve it with what your heart desires.

Nutritional Values: Calories: 133 kcal / Carbohydrates: 4 g / Proteins: 42 g / Fiber: 14 g / Fats: 20 g

Carbohydrates: 25 g / Proteins: 32 g / Fiber: 10 g / Fats: 15 g

CHAPTER 12: Vegetarian

Zucchini Cheesy Lasagna Casserole

Total Time: 1.5 hours/ **Prep. Time:** 15 mins /
Cooking Time: 1 hour / **Difficulty:** Easy
Serving Size: 2 servings

Ingredients:

- 1.2 to 2 pounds of ground low fat turkey meat
- 3- 6oz cans of tomato paste (unless you have your own sauce made up)
- 3 to 4 big zucchinis washed and sliced long ways very thin
- 2 1/2 cups of mozzarella cheese (more if you like it really cheesy)
- 2 cups of cottage cheese (more if you like it cheesy
- 2 eggs
- 1 1/2 cups of water
- Italian herbs to taste
- salt & pepper to taste
- 1/2 cup of parmesan cheese on top
- 1/2 cup of onions chopped fine
- 2 cloves of garlic chopped fine
- 2 tsp trivia (for spaghetti sauce)
- olive oil

Instructions:

Chop your onion and garlic. Cook it and the turkey meat in a little olive oil until browned. Salt and pepper to taste. Slice up the zucchini long ways really thinly. Salt generously and set in a strainer to drain off extra water. Allow zucchini to sit for at least 15 minutes. Place in a dish towel and gently press the excess water out. Mix up the tomato paste with Italian spices, 1 1/2 cups of water. Simmer for 15 minutes. Mix up the cottage cheese, eggs, 1/2 cup of mozzarella cheese with Italian Herbs. Put one small scoop of meat sauce at bottom of pan. Add a layer of zucchini. Add more sauce, then cottage cheese mixture, then mozzarella cheese, then zucchini. Repeat layers until all done. Sprinkle the last of the cheese on top and the pram. Cover with foil and bake for 60 minutes to 330 °F. Enjoy!!

Nutritional Values: Calories: 144 kcal /
Carbohydrates: 28 g / Proteins: 26 g / Fiber: 24 g /
Fats: 10 g

Mushroom Cauliflower Skillet

Total Time: 30 mins / **Prep. Time:** 10 mins /
Cooking Time: 20 mins / **Difficulty:** Easy
Serving Size: 3 servings

Ingredients:

- 1 head of cauliflower, cut into small florets
- 8 oz mushrooms, sliced
- 1 onion, diced
- 2 cloves of garlic, minced
- 2 tbsp olive oil
- Salt and pepper to taste
- 2 tbsp chopped fresh herbs such as parsley, thyme, or dill

Instructions:

In a large skillet, heat the olive oil over medium heat. Add the onion and sauté until softened, about 3-4 minutes. Add the garlic and mushrooms, and sauté for an additional 5 minutes or until mushrooms are softened. Add the cauliflower florets, and stir to combine. Season with salt and pepper. Cover the skillet with a lid and reduce the heat to low. Cook for 10-15 minutes, or until the cauliflower is tender and cooked through. Remove the lid, increase the heat to medium-high and cook for an additional 2-3 minutes, or until any excess liquid has evaporated.

Remove from heat and stir in the fresh herbs. Serve and enjoy.

Nutritional Values: Calories: 89 kcal /
Carbohydrates: 15 g / Proteins: 10 g / Fiber: 26 g /
Fats: 4 g

Vegan Garbanzo Bean Curry

Total Time: 8.5 hours / **Prep. Time:** 10 mins /
Cooking Time: 8 hours / **Difficulty:** Easy
Serving Size: 3 servings

Ingredients:

- 1 1/2 cups Garbanzo Beans
- 1 1/4 cups coarsely chopped onion
- 1/2 cup chopped fresh tomato
- 2 teaspoons minced ginger root
- 2 teaspoons minced garlic
- 1 teaspoon cayenne pepper
- 1 1/2 teaspoons cumin seeds
- 1/2 teaspoon turmeric
- 3/4 teaspoon chili powder
- 2 teaspoons salt
- 1/2 cup thinly sliced green onions (optional)
- 3-4 tablespoons chopped fresh cilantro
- 1 tablespoon fresh squeezed lemon juice

Instructions:
Rinse and sort garbanzos. Using a food processor or the bowl attachment of an immersion blender, puree together onions, tomatoes, ginger, garlic, cayenne, cumin, turmeric, chili powder, and salt. Add the mixture to a slow cooker with the garbanzos and 4 cups of water. Cook on high for about 7 hours, or until garbanzos are soft. Add green onions and cook for additional 60 minutes on high. Stir in chopped cilantro and lemon juice. Serve hot, over rice if desired.

Nutritional Values: Calories: 100 kcal / Carbohydrates: 22 g / Proteins: 42 g / Fiber: 27 g / Fats: 8 g

Spinach & Tomato Frittata

Total Time: 1 hour / **Prep. Time:** 10 mins / **Cooking Time:** 45 mins / **Difficulty:** Easy
Serving Size: 4 servings

Ingredients:
- 8 eggs
- 2 cups spinach, fresh
- 1/3 cups milk
- 4 slices Swiss cheese, diced
- 1 large tomato, diced
- 1 Tbs oil
- Salt & pepper, to taste

Instructions:
Preheat your oven to 350 °F and prepare two 9" pie pans with cooking spray. In a large bowl whisk together the eggs, milk, cheese, tomato and salt & pepper. In a skillet over medium heat add oil and the spinach, cook until wilted; about 7-8 minutes. Once the spinach is cooled 4minutes, add it to the egg mixture and stir to combine. Divide between the mixture between the two pie pans and bake for 30 minutes, until it is set in the center and the edges are golden. Remove carefully from the oven, cool 10 minutes; slice and serve.

Nutritional Values: Calories: 102 kcal / Carbohydrates: 10 g / Proteins: 38 g / Fiber: 32 g / Fats: 12 g

Lemon Chickpea Orzo Soup

Total Time: 30 mins / **Prep. Time:** 5 mins / **Cooking Time:** 25 mins / **Difficulty:** Easy
Serving Size: 4 servings

Ingredients:
- 1 tbsp. olive oil
- 1 onion, diced
- 2 large carrots, halved lengthwise and finely sliced
- 3 celery stalks, chopped
- 3 garlic cloves, minced
- 1/2 tsp. dried thyme
- 4 cups vegetable broth + 1 cup water
- 1 can chickpeas, rinsed and drained
- 1 small sprig rosemary
- Bay leaf
- 1 cup orzo
- 1/8 cup fresh lemon juice

Instructions:
Heat the olive oil over medium heat. Then, add the onion, carrots, celery and garlic. Cook for 8 minutes until vegetables are soft. Next, add the thyme and pinch of pepper; stir together. Then, add the vegetable broth and water and bring to a boil. Add the chickpeas, rosemary, orzo and bay leaf. Reduce heat to a low simmer and cook for 15 minutes until orzo is cooked through. Finally, reduce heat to low and stir in lemon juice.

Nutritional Values: Calories: 109 kcal / Carbohydrates: 42 g / Proteins: 32 g / Fiber: 25 g / Fats: 2 g

Baked Vegan Eggplant & Zucchini Chips

Total Time: 2 hours / **Prep. Time:** 30 mins / **Cooking Time:** 1.5 hour / **Difficulty:** Easy
Serving Size: 5 servings

Ingredients:

- 1-pound small eggplant
- 2 cups zucchini
- Salt, to taste
- 1/2 cup vegan mayonnaise
- 1-1/2 cups panko breadcrumbs
- 2-1/2 teaspoons dried oregano
- 1 teaspoon dried rosemary, crumbled
- Olive oil cooking spray

Instructions:

Preheat oven to 375 °F and lightly oil two large baking sheets. Slice eggplant and zucchini into 1/8-inch, diagonal slices and lightly sprinkle with salt. Arrange on paper towels and let sit for about 45 minutes and blot off any excess moisture. In a shallow bowl, beat vegan mayonnaise with a fork until smooth. In a small baking dish, combine panko crumbs, oregano, and rosemary. Take a slice of eggplant or zucchini and coat both sides with a thin layer of mayonnaise. Dredge each slice generously with herbed panko, and then place in a single layer on baking sheets. Spray with olive oil and bake for 20 minutes, then flip each piece over, spray with more oil, and bake for an additional 10 minutes until panko is golden and crisp. Move to serving platter and serve hot veggie chips immediately with Skordalia.

Nutritional Values: Calories: 99 kcal / Carbohydrates: 10 g / Proteins: 7 g / Fiber: 44 g / Fats: 4 g

Cheesy Broccoli Rice Casserole

Total Time: 40 mins / **Prep. Time:** 10 mins / **Cooking Time:** 30 mins / **Difficulty:** Easy **Serving Size:** 4 servings

Ingredients:

- 1 medium white onion, chopped
- 4 cups fresh broccoli, large stems removed and broken into small pieces
- 1/2 cup (1 stick) unsalted butter
- 1/2 cup milk
- 1 (10.5 ounce) can cream of chicken soup
- 1 cup processed cheese, divided (such as Velveeta)
- 1–1/2 cups quick cooking white rice (about 4 cups cooked)

- 1/3 cup crushed potato chips

Instructions:

Preheat oven to 375 °F. Cook rice according to package directions. Melt butter in a large skillet over medium heat. Add onion and broccoli and cook until onion is transparent. Add soup, 4 ounces cheese and milk. Stir until cheese is melted. Remove from heat and stir in cooked rice. Pour mixture into a lightly greased 8×8-inch casserole dish. Shred or crumble remaining 4 ounces cheese over the top of the mixture and then sprinkle with the crushed potato chips. Bake for 20 minutes until cheese on top is melted and casserole is bubbly.

Nutritional Values: Calories: 109 kcal / Carbohydrates: 39 g / Proteins: 21 g / Fiber: 13 g / Fats: 10 g

Vegetable Casserole

Total Time: 1.5 hours / **Prep. Time:** 10 mins / **Cooking Time:** 70 mins / **Difficulty:** Easy **Serving Size:** 4 servings

Ingredients:

- 1 medium onion, chopped
- 2 large cloves of garlic, chopped
- 2 zucchinis, sliced
- 2 potatoes, sliced
- 2 summer squashes, sliced
- 3 plum tomatoes, sliced
- salt and pepper
- dried thyme
- fresh rosemary, chopped
- 8 oz shredded Italian cheeses

Instructions:

Sauté the garlic and onions in the olive oil until soft, about 10 minutes. Spray an 8 x 8-inch baking dish with cooking spray. Spread the garlic and onion mixture on the bottom of the pan and then begin to stack your veggie slices vertically. Season generously with salt, pepper, rosemary and thyme. Cover dish with aluminum foil and bake in an oven set at 375 °F for 40 minutes. Uncover and sprinkle on the cheese and then return to the oven for another 30 minutes until the cheese is a golden brown. Serve hot and enjoy those vegetables.

Nutritional Values: Calories: 122 kcal / Carbohydrates: 39 g / Proteins: 17 g / Fiber: 15 g Fats: 9 g

Wasabi Pea Snack Mix

Total Time: 10 hours / **Prep. Time:** 30 mins /
Cooking Time: 1.5 hours / **Difficulty:** Medium
Serving Size: 5 servings

Ingredients:
- 4 cups of wasabi peas
- 2 cups of pretzel sticks
- 2 cups of Chex cereal
- 2 cups of sesame sticks
- 1 cup of peanuts
- 1/2 cup of butter
- 2 tbsp wasabi paste
- 2 tbsp soy sauce
- 1 tsp Worcestershire sauce
- 1 tsp garlic powder
- Salt and pepper to taste

Instructions:
Preheat the oven to 250°F (120°C). In a large bowl, mix together the wasabi peas, pretzel sticks, Chex cereal, sesame sticks, and peanuts. In a small saucepan, melt the butter over medium heat.
Add the wasabi paste, soy sauce, Worcestershire sauce, garlic powder, salt and pepper, and stir to combine. Pour the butter mixture over the snack mix and toss to coat evenly. Spread the mix out on a baking sheet, and bake for 1 hour, stirring every 15 minutes, or until the mix is dry and crispy. Remove from the oven and let it cool completely. Once the mix is cool, store it in an airtight container. Enjoy as a snack anytime you like!

Nutritional Values: Calories: 114 kcal / Carbohydrates: 39 g / Proteins: 19 g / Fiber: 35 g / Fats: 8 g

Healthy Choco Banana Cookies

Total Time: 30 mins / **Prep. Time:** 10 mins /
Cooking Time: 20 mins / **Difficulty:** Easy
Serving Size: 4 servings

Ingredients:
- 1½ cup Oatmeal
- 2 tbsp Cocoa powder
- 2 Bananas
- ⅓ cup Choco chips

Instructions:
Preheat the oven at 350 °F and line a baking tray

with parchment paper. In a mixing bowl, take both the bananas and using a fork mash till there is no lumps. Into that, add oatmeal's (1 cup quick oats + 1/2 cup rolled oats) along with cocoa powder and Choco chips. Gently mix everything. Scoop up 2 tbsp of the mixture and shape into ball. Flatten slightly and place over the baking tray. Similarly make balls from rest mixture, flatten a bit and arrange on the baking tray. Bake for 20 minutes or until set thoroughly. Take out the baking tray from the oven and keep aside for few minutes to cool down completely. Serve as breakfast along with a glass of milk!

Nutritional Values: Calories: 85 kcal / Carbohydrates: 32 g / Proteins: 8 g / Fiber: 9 g / Fats: 7 g

CHAPTER 13: Salad

Modern Taco Salad

Total Time: 5 mins / **Prep. Time:** 5 mins /
Cooking Time: / **Difficulty:** Easy
Serving Size: 5 servings

Ingredients:
- Shredded Kalua pork
- Seasoned, cooked black beans
- Cooked sweet corn (or frozen, thawed)
- Sriracha ranch dressing
- Chopped romaine lettuce
- Shredded Mexican blend of cheeses
- Nacho cheese Doritos or other corn chips
- Fresh garden tomatoes Salsa

Instructions:
If chilled, warm the pork, black beans and corn. Fill a salad bowl or plate most of the way with lettuce. Top with shredded pork, beans, corn, shredded cheese, crushed chips, tomatoes and green onion, avocado, cilantro if desired. Drizzle with Sriracha Ranch Dressing and serve with salsa to add more heat to taste if you like.

Nutritional Values: Calories: 72 kcal /
Carbohydrates: 16 g / Proteins: 8 g / Fiber: 38 g /
Fats: 4 g

Grilled Nectarine Salad

Total Time: 5 mins / **Prep. Time:** 5 mins /
Cooking Time: / **Difficulty:** Easy
Serving Size: 4 servings

Ingredients:
For nectarines
- 2 nectarines, 1-inch-wide slices
- 2 tbsp Olive oil
- Kosher salt and pepper, to taste

For salad
- 2.5 pounds cups baby arugula
- grilled nectarines
- 1/2 cup ricotta salted

For vinaigrette
- 3 tablespoons balsamic vinegar
- 2 teaspoons Truvia Nectar
- 1 teaspoon Dijon mustard
- 1/3 cup extra virgin olive oil
- Kosher salt and pepper, to taste

Instructions:
Lightly glaze each slice of nectarine with olive oil, season with kosher salt and pepper and grill quickly on a hot grill. Set aside. Add all ingredients to a large salad bowl, drizzle with desired amount of vinaigrette and toss to combine. Whisk together vinegar, Truvia nectar and Dijon mustard. While whisking slowly drizzle in olive oil until combined. Season with kosher salt and pepper. Serve.

Nutritional Values: Calories: 88 kcal /
Carbohydrates: 6 g / Proteins: 12 g / Fiber: 38 g /
Fats: 7 g

Lentil Salad

Total Time: 20 mins / **Prep. Time:** 5 mins /
Cooking Time: 15 mins / **Difficulty:** Medium
Serving Size: 6 servings

Ingredients:
- 1 cup brown or green lentils, rinsed and picked over
- 2 cups water or broth
- 1 bay leaf
- 1/2 teaspoon salt
- 1/4 cup diced red onion
- 1/4 cup diced bell pepper
- 1/4 cup chopped fresh parsley
- 2 tablespoons lemon juice
- 2 tablespoons extra-virgin olive oil
- Salt and black pepper, to taste

Instructions:
In a medium saucepan, combine the lentils, water or broth, bay leaf, and 1/2 teaspoon salt. Bring to a boil, then reduce the heat and simmer, uncovered, until the lentils are tender, about 20-25 minutes. Drain and discard the bay leaf. In a large bowl, combine the cooked lentils, red onion, bell pepper, and parsley. In a small bowl, whisk together the lemon juice and olive oil. Pour the dressing over the lentils and toss to combine. Season with salt and pepper to taste.
Cover and refrigerate for at least 30 minutes before serving to allow the flavors to meld.

Nutritional Values: Calories: 101 kcal /
Carbohydrates: 11 g / Proteins: 14 g / Fiber: 36 g /

Fats: 6 g

Thai Cabbage Salad

Total Time: 25 mins / **Prep. Time:** 5 mins /
Cooking Time: / **Difficulty:** Easy
Serving Size: 3 servings

Ingredients:
- 1 Family-Sized Bag of Prepared Coleslaw Mix
- 1 Package of Bean Thread Noodles soaked

For The Dressing:
- 1/3 cup Vegetable Broth, Low-Sodium
- 3 tbsp olive oil
- 2 tbsp Agave Syrup
- 3 tbsp Low Sodium Soy Sauce
- squeeze Fresh Lime Juice
- 1/2 tsp Sesame Oil
- 1 Clove Garlic minced

For Garnish:
- Handful fresh Cilantro or parsley if you prefer
- 2 tbsp Peanuts chopped
- Lime Wedgesù

Instructions:
The cellophane noodles need to be soaked in hot water for 15 minutes and then drained thoroughly. If desired, cut the noodles into smaller pieces using kitchen shears. You can also break the noodles prior to soaking. Creamy peanut butter is whisked together with vegetable broth and agave syrup for a bit of sweetness. Add soy sauce, sesame oil, minced garlic and a squeeze of fresh lime juice. Add the slaw mixture to the dressing along with the drained noodles. Toss together to combine. Garnish with fresh cilantro. Serve with lime wedges.

Nutritional Values: Calories: 79 kcal /
Carbohydrates: 10 g / Proteins: 7 g / Fiber: 32 g /
Fats: 5 g

Moroccan Rice Salad

Total Time: 10 mins / **Prep. Time:** 10 mins /
Cooking Time: / **Difficulty:** Easy
Serving Size: 5 servings

Ingredients:

- 1/4 cup chopped fresh parsley
- 1/3 cup chopped fresh cilantro
- 1/4 cup chopped fresh mint
- 1/2 cup chopped scallions
- 1/4 cup chopped red onion
- chopped green bell pepper
- 1/4 cup chopped carrots
- 2 tablespoons olive oil
- 1 3/4 cups cooked white rice
- 1/2 cup raisins
- 2 tablespoons lemon juice
- 2 cloves garlic, minced
- 1 teaspoon ground cumin
- Salt and pepper, to taste

Instructions:
In a large bowl, combine the cooked rice, raisins, parsley, cilantro, mint, scallions, red onion, bell peppers, and carrots. In a small bowl, whisk together the olive oil, lemon juice, garlic, cumin, salt, and pepper. Pour the dressing over the rice mixture and toss to combine. Chill the salad in the refrigerator for at least 1 hour before serving.

Nutritional Values: Calories: 92 kcal /
Carbohydrates: 38 g / Proteins: 14 g / Fiber: 35 g /
Fats: 5 g

Steak Salad

Total Time: 30 mins / **Prep. Time:** 10 mins /
Cooking Time: 10 mins / **Difficulty:** Easy
Serving Size: 6 servings

Ingredients:
- 1 lb sirloin steak
- Salt and pepper
- 2 tbsp olive oil
- 8 cups mixed salad greens
- 1/2 cup cherry tomatoes, halved
- 1/2 red onion, thinly sliced
- 1/2 cup crumbled blue cheese
- 2 tbsp balsamic vinegar
- 2 tbsp olive oil
- 1 clove garlic, minced
- Salt and pepper, to taste

Instructions:

Season the steak with salt and pepper. Heat 1 tablespoon of olive oil in a large skillet over medium-high heat. Add the steak and cook for about 3-5 minutes per side for medium-rare, or until desired level of doneness. Remove the steak from the skillet and let it rest for about 5 minutes. In a large bowl, combine the salad greens, cherry tomatoes, and red onion. In a small bowl, whisk together the balsamic vinegar, remaining olive oil, and minced garlic. Season with salt and pepper to taste. Thinly slice the rested steak and add it to the bowl with the salad greens.

Add the dressing to the bowl and toss to combine. Add the blue cheese to the bowl and toss again. Divide the salad among plates and serve.

Nutritional Values: Calories: 103 kcal / Carbohydrates: 9 g / Proteins: 38 g / Fiber: 35 g / Fats: 8 g

Roasted Sweet Potato

Total Time: 60 mins / **Prep. Time:** 10 mins / **Cooking Time:** 45 mins / **Difficulty:** Medium
Serving Size: 5 servings

Ingredients:
- 1 3/4 cups cooked black beans
- 1 bell pepper, seeded and diced, about 1.25 cups
- 4 cups pounds sweet potatoes, peeled
- 1 hot Chile, seeded if you are sensitive to heat
- 1 cup (heaping) chopped fresh cilantro
- 3 limes, juiced to yield about 6 tablespoons
- 1 large red onion, diced to yield about 2 cups
- $^1/_2$ cup extra-virgin olive oil
- Kosher salt and pepper to taste
- 1 clove garlic

Instructions:
Cut the potatoes in 1-inch cubes. Heat oven to 385 °F. Put sweet potatoes on one half of a rimmed sheet pan and toss with olive oil. Put onions on other half of pan and toss with another tablespoon of olive oil. Spread vegetables out in a single layer. Season all over with salt and pepper. Roast for 45 minutes, checking after 20 to ensure everything is browning properly. Remove pan from oven. Put chilies in a blender or mini food processor along with garlic, lime juice, remaining 6 tablespoons of olive oil and a sprinkle of salt and pepper. Process until blended. Mixture will taste super tart. Before you adjust the seasoning, proceed to next step. Put warm

vegetables in a large bowl with beans and bell pepper; toss with dressing and cilantro. Taste and adjust seasoning if necessary. Serve warm or at room temperature or refrigerate for up to a day.

Nutritional Values: Calories: 114 kcal / Carbohydrates: 45 g / Proteins: 22 g / Fiber: 38 g / Fats: 8 g

Taco Salad

Total Time: 20 mins / **Prep. Time:** 5 mins / **Cooking Time:** / **Difficulty:** Easy
Serving Size: 4 servings

Ingredients:
- 1 Head Lettuce shredded
- 2 cups bottle Catalina dressing
- 2-3 tomatoes chopped
- 1 onion chopped, if desired
- 2 cups shredded cheddar cheese
- 1 1/2 lbs. hamburger browned, and grease drained off
- 1 ¾ cups bag Nacho Cheese Doritos crushed

Instructions:
Brown hamburger and drain off grease. Mix it together with lettuce, dressing, tomatoes, onion and cheddar cheese in large bowl. Refrigerate until ready to serve. Right before serving mix in Doritos.

Nutritional Values: Calories: 85 kcal / Carbohydrates: 24 g / Proteins: 18 g / Fiber: 25 g / Fats: 5 g

Cucumber Watermelon Summer Salad

Total Time: 40 mins / **Prep. Time:** 5 mins / **Cooking Time:** / **Difficulty:** Easy
Serving Size: 5 servings

Ingredients:

- 4 cups cubed seedless watermelon
- 1 large cucumber, peeled, seeded and diced
- 1/4 cup chopped fresh mint
- 2 tbsp fresh lime juice
- 1 tbsp honey
- Salt and pepper, to taste
- Crumbled feta cheese, for garnish (optional)

Instructions:
In a large bowl, combine the cubed watermelon, diced cucumber, and chopped mint. In a small bowl, whisk together the lime juice and honey. Season with salt and pepper to taste. Pour the dressing over the watermelon mixture, and toss gently to coat. Cover and refrigerate for at least 30 minutes to allow the flavors to meld. Before serving, top with crumbled feta cheese if desired.

Nutritional Values: Calories: 84 kcal / Carbohydrates: 10 g / Proteins: 7 g / Fiber: 39 g / Fats: 6 g

Pineapple Cucumber Lime Salad

Total Time: 5 mins / **Prep. Time:** 5 mins / **Cooking Time:** / **Difficulty:** Easy
Serving Size: 4 servings

Ingredients:
- 1 pineapple chopped
- 1 English cucumber chopped
- 3 limes zested and juiced
- 1/4 cup cilantro roughly chopped
- salt and pepper optional

Instructions:
Combine all ingredients and toss lightly to distribute the lime juice and zest evenly. Season with salt and pepper if desired. Serve immediately or keep chilled until ready to serve.

Nutritional Values: Calories: 68 kcal / Carbohydrates: 4 g / Proteins: 3 g / Fiber: 28 g / Fats: 0 g

Clean Eating Taco Salad

Total Time: 15 mins / **Prep. Time:** 5 mins / **Cooking Time:** 10 mins / **Difficulty:** Easy
Serving Size: 4 servings

Ingredients:

- 2 cups lean ground turkey optional beef
- 3 tablespoons taco seasoning homemade, or store bought
- 1-pound tomatoes fresh, chopped
- 1.5 cup cheddar reduced fat, grated
- 3.5 pounds lettuce shredded or thinly sliced
- 1 cup guacamole homemade or store bought
- 1/2 cup salsa or enchilada sauce, homemade or store bought

Instructions:
Cook meat in a skillet over medium heat until browned, for about 10 minutes, stirring frequently. Drain any fat and add taco seasoning, and 1/3 cup water. Cook for an additional 2 minutes, stirring frequently. Arrange 4 plates and top with an even amount of tomatoes, lettuce, cheese, guacamole, and salsa. If desired, add a dollop of Greek yogurt or sour cream. Enjoy!

Nutritional Values: Calories: 72 kcal / Carbohydrates: 30 g / Proteins: 17 g / Fiber: 34 g / Fats: 5 g

CHAPTER 14: Snack

Baked Herbed Spiral Fries

Total Time: 30 mins / **Prep. Time:** 10 mins / **Cooking Time:** 20 mins / **Difficulty:** Easy **Serving Size:** 4 servings

Ingredients:
- 2 sweet potatoes
- 2 Tbsp. oil
- 1/3 tsp. ground cumin
- 1/4 tsp. chipotle chili powder
- 1/2 tsp. kosher salt
- 1/3 tsp. pepper
- ½ pound light mayonnaise
- 3 chipotles in adobo
- 1 Tbsp. lime juice

Instructions:
Trim the ends off potatoes and cut to fit spiralizer attachment. Use the spiral slice blade (small core) and peeling blade to make potato spirals. Cut spirals into individual rounds by cutting through one side of the spiral. Soak potatoes in a bowl of cold water for 65 minutes to remove some starch. Drain and rinse the potato rounds and spread out on a clean kitchen towel. Pat the tops dry with another towel. Preheat oven to 380 °F. Arrange two oven racks to the bottom and upper thirds of the oven. Drizzle a teaspoon of oil onto each of two large baking sheets. Rub the oil around with a paper towel. Place baking sheets in oven to preheat. Cook for 20 minutes and serve.

Nutritional Values: Calories: 104 kcal / Carbohydrates: 10 g / Proteins: 12 g / Fiber: 7 g / Fats: 9 g

Edamame Hummus

Total Time: 5 mins / **Prep. Time:** 5 mins / **Cooking Time:** / **Difficulty:** Easy **Serving Size:** 4 servings

Ingredients:
- 2 cups shelled edamame fully steamed
- 2 cloves garlic minced
- 1/3 cup lemon juice
- 1/2 cup tahini
- 1/3 cup olive oil

- 1 teaspoon kosher salt

Instructions:
In a food processor, thoroughly blend your edamame. Make sure it is as smooth as possible, scraping down the sides to ensure all of it is smooth. Add in the remaining ingredients and blend until smooth. If needed add more olive oil and lemon juice until the edamame is completely smooth.

Nutritional Values: Calories: 100 kcal / Carbohydrates: 24 g / Proteins: 18 g / Fiber: 20 g / Fats: 10 g

Cookies and Cream Cheesecake Cupcakes

Total Time: 45 mins / **Prep. Time:** 10 mins / **Cooking Time:** 30 mins / **Difficulty:** Easy **Serving Size:** 6 servings

Ingredients:
- 21 Oreo cookies
- 1 pound cream cheese, at room temperature
- 1/3 cup granulated sugar
- 1/2 teaspoon vanilla extract
- 2 large eggs
- 1/3 cup sour cream
- Salt

Instructions:
Preheat the oven to 250 °F. Line 2 standard muffin tins with 15 paper liners. Place 1 whole Oreo cookie in the bottom of each lined cup. In a large bowl, use an electric mixer to beat the cream cheese until smooth. Add the sugar and beat until combined. Beat in the vanilla then add the eggs, one at a time, beating until combined. Beat in the sour cream and salt. Do not overmix. Stir in the chopped Oreo cookies. Divide the batter among the cookie-lined cups, filling each almost to the top. Bake until the filling is set, about 25 minutes. Transfer to wire racks to cool completely inside the muffin tins. Refrigerate at least 2 hours before serving.

Nutritional Values: Calories: 143 kcal / Carbohydrates: 34 g / Proteins: 9 g / Fiber: 4 g / Fats: 12 g

Chocolate Black Bean Brownie Bites

Total Time: 60 mins / **Prep. Time:** 20 mins / **Cooking Time:** 30 mins / **Difficulty:** Easy
Serving Size: 3 servings

Ingredients:
- 3 tbsp cocoa powder
- 1 tbsp Dutch cocoa powder, or additional regular
- 1/2 cup oats, or 1/2 cup almond flour
- 1 can black beans, or 1 1/2 cup cooked
- 1/4 tsp salt
- 1/2 cup pure maple syrup, honey, or agave
- 1/4 cup oil
- 2 tsp pure vanilla extract
- 1/3 tsp baking powder
- 1/2 cup mini chocolate chips, or more for garnish

Instructions:
Preheat oven to 330 °F. Grease a mini muffin pan. Process all ingredients except chips in a high-quality food processor until smooth. Stir in chips. Portion into the pan, press a few more chips into the tops if desired, and bake on the center rack 15 minutes. Remove from the oven and let cool at least 15 additional minutes before going around the sides with a knife and popping out.

Nutritional Values: Calories: 104 kcal / Carbohydrates: 40 g / Proteins: 14 g / Fiber: 6 g / Fats: 6 g

Crispy Kale Chips

Total Time: 5 mins / **Prep. Time:** 5 mins / **Cooking Time:** / **Difficulty:** Easy
Serving Size: 4 servings

Ingredients:
- 1 Head of Kale
- 1 Tablespoon of Olive Oil
- 2 Teaspoons of Soya Sauce

Instructions:
Remove the center steam of the kale. Tear the kale up into 1 1/2" pieces. Wash clean and dry thoroughly. Toss with the olive oil and soya sauce. Fry in the air fryer at 180 °F for 5-7 minutes, tossing the leaves halfway through. Enjoy!

Nutritional Values: Calories: 98 kcal / Carbohydrates: 12 g / Proteins: 5 g / Fiber: 27 g /

Fats: 2 g

Peanut Butter Protein Bites

Total Time: 5 mins / **Prep. Time:** 5 mins / **Cooking Time:** / **Difficulty:** Easy
Serving Size: 4 servings

Ingredients:
- 1 3/4 cups rolled oats
- ½ pound seed oil
- ½ cup raw honey
- ½ cup raw sunflower seeds
- ½ cup mini chocolate chips
- 2 tbsp. chia seeds

Instructions:
Add all ingredients to a food processor and pulse until well combined. Cover and refrigerate mixture for 60 minutes. Form 1.5" balls and place on a baking sheet lined with waxed paper. Refrigerate for at least 45 minutes. Enjoy!

Nutritional Values: Calories: 155 kcal / Carbohydrates: 39 g / Proteins: 14 g / Fiber: 4 g / Fats: 22 g

Healthy Avocado Toast

Total Time: 10 mins / **Prep. Time:** 5 mins / **Cooking Time:** 5 mins / **Difficulty:** Easy
Serving Size: 2 servings

Ingredients:
- 1 avocado, ripe (but not over ripe)
- ½ lime
- 4 slices of crusty bread, each about 1" thick
- Olive oil
- Flaky sea salt

Instructions:
Preheat your grill. Cut the avocado in half, remove the seed and using a spoon scoop both halves of the avocado into a bowl. Using a fork, gently mash the avocado until slightly chunky. Add a squeeze of lime juice and mix lightly. Brush both sides of each slice of bread with olive oil and place on the grill. Grill on both sides until golden brown and even slightly charred. Remove from grill and spread ¼ of the mashed avocado on each slice. Sprinkle generously with sea salt, then add the shichimi togarashi.

Nutritional Values: Calories: 100 kcal / Carbohydrates: 38 g / Proteins: 12 g / Fiber: 9 g / Fats: 4 g

Toasted Rosemary Walnuts

Total Time: 5 mins / **Prep. Time:** 5 mins / **Cooking Time:** / **Difficulty:** Easy
Serving Size: 4 servings

Ingredients:
- 1-pound raw walnuts
- 1 oz fresh rosemary chopped finely chopped finely.
- 1/3 cup olive oil
- 1/2 teaspoon salt
- 1 teaspoon pepper

Instructions:
Preheat oven to 300 °F and line a baking sheet with parchment paper or a silpat baking sheet
In a bowl whisk together olive oil, rosemary, salt, pepper. Add in walnuts and toss until completely covered in olive oil mixture. Bake the walnuts for 20-25 minutes in the oven, tossing every 10 minutes until they are golden brown. The walnuts cook quickly- so be careful not to burn them!

Nutritional Values: Calories: 104 kcal / Carbohydrates: 40 g / Proteins: 5 g / Fiber: 17 g / Fats: 6 g

Healthy Homemade Trail Mix

Total Time: 5 mins / **Prep. Time:** 5 mins / **Cooking Time:** / **Difficulty:** Easy
Serving Size: 5 servings

Ingredients:
- 1/2 cup cereal such as Cheerios, Wheat Chex, or Barbara's Puffins
- 2/3 cup whole-grain pretzels (or GF for gluten-free option)
- 1/2 cup favorite nuts (almonds, cashews, peanuts, walnuts, etc.)
- 1/3 cup seeds such as pepitas or sunflower
- 1 cup dried fruit such as raisins, chopped dried apricots, dried cherries, or dried apples
- 1/4 cup dark chocolate chips (optional)

Instructions:
Put all ingredients together in a large bowl and use your hands or a spoon to combine. Transfer to an airtight container or resealable bag.

Nutritional Values: Calories: 100 kcal / Carbohydrates: 15 g / Proteins: 5 g / Fiber: 4 g / Fats: 6 g

Baked Crack Chicken Casserole

Total Time: 60 mins / **Prep. Time:** 10 mins / **Cooking Time:** 45 mins / **Difficulty:** Easy
Serving Size: 5 servings

Ingredients:
- 2.5-pound chicken cooked, cubed or shredded
- 1 ounce Ranch dressing mix
- 1 cup bacon cooked and chopped
- ½ pound cheddar cheese shredded
- 1 cup sour cream
- 1.5 cups cream of chicken soup
- 1 and ½ cups butter crackers crushed
- ¼ cup butter melted

Instructions:
Preheat oven to 300 °F. Spray 9x9-inch oven-safe dish with non-stick spray. Combine chicken, ranch mix, cheese, bacon, sour cream, and cream of chicken soup. Stir. Spread in prepared pan.
Combine crushed crackers and melted butter. Sprinkle over chicken. Bake 45 minutes, until heated through and crackers are toasted on top. Serve hot.

Nutritional Values: Calories: 114 kcal / Carbohydrates: 34 g / Proteins: 42 g / Fiber: 4 g / Fats: 8 g

Salmon with Smoky Mayo & Quinoa Pilaf

Total Time: 45 mins / **Prep. Time:** 15 mins / **Cooking Time:** 30 mins / **Difficulty:** Easy
Serving Size: 4 servings

Ingredients:
- 4 frozen salmon fillets
- 5 oz quinoa
- 1/8 cup mayonnaise
- 1 teaspoon smoked paprika
- 1 teaspoon grated garlic, divided
- ½ cup panko breadcrumbs
- 2 tablespoons extra-virgin olive oil, divided
- ¼ teaspoon salt, divided
- 2 cups frozen peas
- ½ teaspoon dried dill
- ½ teaspoon lemon zest
- 1 tablespoon lemon juice

Instructions:
Preheat oven to 375 °F. Bring water to a boil in a

medium saucepan. Place salmon in a baking dish. Cover tightly with foil. Bake for 20-30 minutes. Meanwhile, add quinoa to the boiling water, cover and reduce heat to maintain a lively simmer. Cook until most of the water has been absorbed and the quinoa is tender. Combine mayonnaise, paprika and 1/4 teaspoon garlic in a small bowl. Combine panko, 1 tablespoon oil, 1/8 teaspoon salt and 1/2 teaspoon garlic in another small bowl. Uncover the salmon and spread each fillet with about 1 tablespoon of the mayonnaise mixture topped with 2 tablespoons of the panko mixture, pressing to adhere. Continue baking, uncovered, until the fish is opaque in the center and the breadcrumbs are golden brown, 8-12 minutes more. Add peas and the remaining 1/2 teaspoon garlic, 1 tablespoon oil and 1/8 teaspoon salt to the quinoa. Cook over medium heat, stirring, until the peas are hot, and the water is mostly evaporated, about 2 minutes. Stir in dill, lemon zest and lemon juice. Serve the quinoa with the salmon.

Nutritional Values: Calories: 135 kcal / Carbohydrates: 38 g / Proteins: 27 g / Fiber: 18 g / Fats: 9 g

Snow Pea & Carrot Salad with Miso-Tamari Dressing

Total Time: 30 mins / **Prep. Time:** 10 mins / **Cooking Time:** 15 mins / **Difficulty:** Easy **Serving Size:** 4 servings

Ingredients:
- 2 cups fresh or frozen medium shrimp in shells
- ½ cup reduced-sodium chicken broth
- 1 tablespoon reduced-sodium soy sauce
- 3 teaspoons cornstarch
- 2.5 teaspoons grated fresh ginger
- 2.5 teaspoons sesame oil
- 2 cloves garlic, minced
- A pinch salt
- ¼ teaspoon crushed red pepper (Optional)
- 2 tablespoons vegetable oil
- ½ pound sliced onion
- 1 cup packaged fresh julienned carrots
- 12 ounces snow pea pods, trimmed
- 1 cups hot cooked brown rice

Instructions:
Thaw shrimp, if frozen. Peel and devein shrimp, leaving tails intact if desired. Rinse shrimp; pat dry. In a small bowl combine chicken broth, soy sauce, cornstarch, ginger, oil, garlic, salt and crushed red pepper. In a 12-inch skillet or a wok heat vegetable oil over medium-high. Add onion and carrots; cook and stir 5minutes or just until beginning to soften. Add pea pods; cook and stir 5 minutes. Add shrimp; cook and stir 2 minutes more or just until shrimp are opaque. Add sauce; cook and stir until thick and bubbly. Serve shrimp mixture over rice.

Nutritional Values: Calories: 104 kcal / Carbohydrates: 24 g / Proteins: 25 g / Fiber: 14 g / Fats: 10 g

Mediterranean Roasted Chickpeas

Total Time: 60 mins / **Prep. Time:** 20 mins / **Cooking Time:** 35 mins / **Difficulty:** Easy **Serving Size:** 5 servings

Ingredients:
- 2 15 oz Cans Chickpeas
- 3 Tbsp Extra Virgin Olive Oil
- 2 tsp Red Wine Vinegar
- 2 tsp Fresh Lemon Juice
- A pinch Kosher Salt
- 1 tsp Dried Oregano
- 1/3 tsp Garlic Powder
- 1 tsp Cracked Black Pepper

Instructions:
Preheat oven to 390 °F and line a baking sheet with parchment paper. Drain, rinse, and thoroughly dry the chickpeas, then place in a single layer on the baking sheet. Roast for 15 minutes, then remove from oven, use a spatula to turn the chickpeas so they bake evenly, then roast for another 5 minutes. In a large mixing bowl, add the remaining ingredients and whisk to combine. Add the hot chickpeas and toss gently until fully coated. Place the coated chickpeas back onto the baking sheet and continue roasting for 15 more minutes, checking occasionally to be ensure they don't overcook and burn. Allow to cool completely and enjoy!

Nutritional Values: Calories: 80 kcal / Carbohydrates: 40 g / Proteins: 32 g / Fiber: 46 g / Fats: 6 g

Roasted Carrots

Total Time: 5 mins / **Prep. Time:** 5 mins /

Cooking Time: / **Difficulty:** Easy
Serving Size: 4 servings

Ingredients:
- 6 whole carrots
- olive oil spray
- Salt
- 3 sprigs rosemary (minced)
- 4 sprig thyme

Instructions:
Preheat oven to 400 °F. Spray a roasting pan or cookie sheet with olive oil spray. Cut the carrots in half. Cut the halved carrots in half again lengthwise. Spread the carrots out on the pan. Spray carrots with more olive oil spray. Sprinkle with the salt and herbs. Roast for about 35 minutes, turning at least once

Nutritional Values: Calories: 77 kcal / Carbohydrates: 6 g / Proteins: 3 g / Fiber: 38 g / Fats: 1 g

Crispy Roasted Chickpeas

Total Time: 60 mins / **Prep. Time:** 5 mins / **Cooking Time:** 50 mins / **Difficulty:** Easy
Serving Size: 5 servings

Ingredients:
- 1-pound boiled chickpeas
- 2 teaspoons olive oil
- 1 teaspoon paprika
- 1 teaspoon salt
- ½ teaspoon cumin

Instructions:
Preheat oven at 385 °F. Using a kitchen towel or paper towel, pat dry the chickpeas until they are as dry as possible. Transfer the chickpeas on a baking sheet. Roast them in oven for 20 minutes. Take them from the oven. Drizzle olive oil on the chickpeas and mix them around with your hands so that they are all evenly coated. Sprinkle salt, paprika and cumin and repeat the same step. Make sure they are all evenly coated with these spices. Place back in the oven and roast for another 20 minutes. Check them after 10 minutes and if they are not crispy enough, bake for another 10 minutes.

Nutritional Values: Calories: 90 kcal / Carbohydrates: 25 g / Proteins: 25 g / Fiber: 41 g / Fats: 2 g

Tropical Green Juice

Total Time: 5 mins / **Prep. Time:** 5 mins / **Cooking Time:** / **Difficulty:** Easy
Serving Size: 3 servings

Ingredients:
- 5 oz fresh pineapple juice
- 5 oz fresh spinach juice
- 1/2 cup fresh mango juice
- 1 oz fresh lime juice

Instructions:
Stir juices together thoroughly, divide between two glasses, and serve immediately.

Nutritional Values: Calories: 55 kcal / Carbohydrates: 4 g / Proteins: 0 g / Fiber: 2 g / Fats: 0 g

White Bean Hummus

Total Time: 5 mins / **Prep. Time:** 5 mins / **Cooking Time:** / **Difficulty:** Easy
Serving Size: 4 servings

Ingredients:
- 1 can white beans, drained and rinsed
- 3 cloves garlic
- 2 tablespoons fresh lemon juice
- 1/2 teaspoon salt
- 1 tablespoon olive oil
- 2 leaves fresh basil, diced
- 4 leaves fresh oregano, diced
- 1 tablespoon olive oil

Instructions:
With an immersion blender or food processor, mix beans, garlic, lemon juice, salt and olive oil until smooth. In small skillet heat over medium heat until hot. Serve on a plate, drizzle olive oil on top and add herbs, salt, and pepper. Serve with toasted bread or chips. Great on veggie sandwiches too.

Nutritional Values: Calories: 95 kcal / Carbohydrates: 6 g / Proteins: 18 g / Fiber: 25 g / Fats: 2 g

CHAPTER 15: Soup

Lemon Chicken Orzo Soup

Total Time: 50 mins / **Prep. Time:** 20 mins / **Cooking Time:** 30 mins / **Difficulty:** Easy
Serving Size: 3 servings

Ingredients:

Seasonings
- 1 teaspoon dried oregano
- 1 teaspoon dried basil
- 1.5 teaspoon dried parsley
- 1 teaspoon mustard powder
- ½ teaspoon dried dill weed

Chicken
- 2.5 tablespoons olive oil
- 1   ¼ lbs. boneless   skinless   chicken breast, see notes
- Lemon Pepper Seasoning

Soup
- ½ cup dry white wine, see notes
- 2 tablespoons butter
- 1/2 teaspoon hot sauce
- 1 teaspoon Worcestershire sauce
- ½ cup heavy cream
- 1 3/4 cups fresh spinach
- ½ cup Parmesan cheese, freshly grated
- Juice of 1 lemon, (3-4 Tbsp.)
- 1 small yellow onion, diced
- ¾ cup carrots, diced
- 2.5 sticks celery
- 4 cloves garlic
- 6 cups chicken broth
- ¾ cup orzo, uncooked

Instructions:

Heat olive oil over medium-high heat. **Season the chicken with lemon pepper seasoning** and add it to the heated pot. Sear on each side for 6 minutes, until a golden color has developed. Remove and let rest for 5 minutes, then dice (or shred) into bite-sized pieces. **Add white wine** to the skillet over medium heat and use a silicone spatula to "clean" the bottom of the pot. Bring it to a gentle bubble and let it simmer for 5 minutes, or until reduced by half. **Add the butter along with the onions, carrots, and celery.** Soften for 5 minutes, then **add the garlic** and cook for 60 seconds. **Add the seasonings, hot sauce,** and **Worcestershire sauce** and toss to coat. **Add the chicken broth.** Bring to a boil, then reduce to a simmer. **Add the chicken back** and simmer gently until cooked through. The soup will continue to reduce and concentrate the longer it simmers. While the soup simmers, **boil the orzo** in a separate pot of salted water according to package instructions. Drain once cooked. Reduce heat of the soup to low and **stir in the heavy cream**. Gradually **sprinkle in the Parmesan cheese,** stirring continuously. **Add the spinach** and let it heat through for 4 minutes, or until wilted. Remove from heat. **Stir in the lemon juice. Add cooked orzo** to serving bowls and ladle the soup on top. Serve

Nutritional Values: Calories: 109 kcal / Carbohydrates: 36 g / Proteins: 42 g / Fiber: 18 g / Fats: 8 g

Coconut Curry Carrot and Sweet Potato Soup

Total Time: 40 mins / **Prep. Time:** 10 mins / **Cooking Time:** 30 mins / **Difficulty:** Easy
Serving Size: 4 servings

Ingredients:
- 6 carrots
- 1 sweet potatoes
- 2.5 cups vegetable stock
- 2 Tbsp. green curry paste (or red curry paste; Thai style)
- 2 tsp. curry powder (yellow)
- salt and ground black pepper (freshly ground, to taste)
- 1 Tbsp. coconut oil
- 1 yellow onion (diced)
- 1 pinch salt
- 1 lime (juice)
- 2 cups coconut milk
- roasted cashews (bits, to garnish, optional)
- cilantro

Instructions:
Add the coconut oil in a saucepan and heat over medium heat. Add the onion and a pinch of salt and cook for 3 minutes, stirring frequently. Add the carrots, sweet potatoes, vegetable stock, curry paste, curry powder, salt, and freshly ground black pepper (to taste) to the saucepan and bring to a boil over medium-high heat. Cover and reduce to low and simmer for 25 minutes. The vegetables should be very tender. Add the carrot and sweet potato mixture, lime juice, and coconut milk in a blender and secure the lid on top. Turn the dial to Speed 1

and slowly increase to Speed 5 or 6 and blend until smooth for 90 seconds. Steam should be visible. Serve immediately, topping with cashew bits and cilantro.

Nutritional Values: Calories: 100 kcal / Carbohydrates: 34 g / Proteins: 22 g / Fiber: 16 g / Fats: 7 g

Soup Minestrones

Total Time: 60 mins / **Prep. Time:** 15 mins / **Cooking Time:** 45 mins / **Difficulty:** Easy
Serving Size: 7 servings

Ingredients:
- 1 small onion, about 1/3 cup, diced
- 2 cloves garlic, minced
- 1 medium carrot
- 1 medium zucchini (around 2/3 cups), sliced into halves or quarters
- 1/3 cup cooked red kidney beans
- 1/3 cup canned or cooked cannellini beans
- 1/4 cup dried gluten-free small shell pasta
- 3/4 cup fresh baby spinach chopped, optional
- 1/2 - 1 teaspoon balsamic vinegar, optional but adds great flavor
- 1 large celery stalk
- 3 teaspoons dried basil
- 1.5 teaspoon dried oregano
- 3/4 teaspoon dried thyme
- 1 32 oz can dice tomatoes
- 3 tablespoons tomato paste
- 1 bay leaf
- 1 (32 oz carton - 4 cups) low sodium vegetable broth
- Shredded or grated Parmesan cheese
- Fresh parsley finely chopped

Instructions:
In a large heavy bottomed pot or Dutch oven, heat olive oil over medium heat. Add onions, garlic, carrots and celery and sauté for about 6 minutes, or until vegetables are slightly softened. Add basil, oregano and thyme and cook for an additional 60 seconds. Add the diced tomatoes, tomato paste, bay leaf, vegetable broth and both of the beans. Depending on how large your pot is, add just enough water to cover the vegetables. Bring soup to a boil, then reduce heat and allow to simmer for 35-40 minutes. Stir in the dried pasta shells and zucchini and cook for another 5 minutes, or until pasta is cooked. Stir in the spinach and allow to wilt.

Add more water as needed if you like a thinner soup. Season with more salt and pepper as needed and stir in balsamic vinegar (if using). Serve warm with bread and top with Parmesan cheese and garnish with parsley if desired.

Nutritional Values: Calories: 98 kcal / Carbohydrates: 32 g / Proteins: 13 g / Fiber: 14 g / Fats: 3 g

Farmers Market Ramen

Total Time: 50 mins / **Prep. Time:** 10 mins / **Cooking Time:** 40 mins / **Difficulty:** Easy
Serving Size: 6 servings

Ingredients:
- 2.5 pounds ramen noodles
- 6.5-pound ramen stock
- 4 large eggs
- 1 cup grape tomatoes, roasted
- 1/2 cup olive oil
- 1 pound corn kernels
- 1 cup zucchini, diced
- ½ pound yellow squash, diced
- 1 cup carrots, diced
- 8.33 oz red onion, sliced thinly
- 4 jalapenos, sliced into rounds

Instructions:
Preheat oven to 385 °F. Place tomatoes on a baking sheet with salt, pepper, and drizzle of olive oil. Roast tomatoes for about 25 minutes or until blistered. Remove from oven and set aside. In a large skillet preheat to medium-high heat add the olive oil, zucchini, squash, carrots, red onion, corn, salt and pepper. Sauté until all the veggies have softened about 12 minutes. Add more olive oil making sure nothing sticks to the skillet. Set veggies aside. Fill a stock pot with water and bring to a boil Gently add the eggs to the water and set a timer for seven minutes. Then move the eggs to an ice bath to cool completely. Once cooled, crack the egg slightly and remove the shell. Slice in half when ready to serve. In a large stock pot, add the ramen stock. Bring to a boil. Add the ramen without the seasonings to the pot. Cook for about 5 minutes or until ramen has cooked through. To serve, divide ramen between four bowls. Ladle the stock into the bowls. Divide the veggie mixture between the bowls and garnish with jalapeños. Place sliced eggs on top. Serve immediately

Nutritional Values: Calories: 146 kcal / Carbohydrates: 42 g / Proteins: 12 g / Fiber: 8 g /

Fats: 5 g

Coconut Lentil Stew with Kale

Total Time: 60 mins / **Prep. Time:** 10 mins / **Cooking Time:** 45 mins / **Difficulty:** Easy
Serving Size: 6 servings

Ingredients:
- 1/2 Tbs curry paste
- 1 3/4 cups red lentils
- 1/2 yellow onion
- 1-2 garlic cloves, minced
- 2.5 cups kale, chopped
- 1 tsp ground cumin
- 1 pound lite coconut milk
- 2 cups tomato sauce
- 1 cube (2 oz) vegetable bouillon
- Salt and black pepper to taste
- Additional optional vegetables: bell pepper, mushrooms, squash, carrots

Instructions:
In a large stovetop pot on high heat, add in the onion and garlic. Cook for 5-6 minutes and add in a splash of water to prevent burning. Then add the curry paste. If sautéing additional vegetables, add in now and cook for 10-12 minutes. Add in the lentils and stir for 60 seconds. Then, add in the coconut milk, tomato sauce, vegetable bouillon, and seasoning. Bring the mixture to a boil cooking on medium-medium/high, stirring frequently to prevent the stew from sticking to the bottom. Once boiling, reduce heat to low and simmer. Cover with a lid. Cook the stew for another 20 minutes, stirring occasionally. Add about 1/4-1/2 more water if needed if the stew is too thick. Then, add the kale to the top of the stew. Do not stir it in. Cover with a lid and allow it to wilt for 3 minutes. Then, stir in and remove the stew from heat. Serve fresh and enjoy.

Nutritional Values: Calories: 121 kcal / Carbohydrates: 38 g / Proteins: 18 g / Fiber: 45 g / Fats: 5 g

Lamb Stew

Total Time: 2.5 hours/ **Prep. Time:** 20 mins / **Cooking Time:** 2 hours / **Difficulty:** Easy
Serving Size: 7 servings

Ingredients:
- 1.5 tablespoons olive oil
- ⅓ cup flour
- 2 pounds leftover lamb (cut into 1" cubes)
- 3 cups small new baby potatoes (halved or quartered bit-sized pieces)
- 3.5 cups lamb stock
- 2 large tomatoes (½" chopped)
- 2 tablespoons tomato paste
- 1 tablespoon fresh thyme (or 1 to 2 teaspoons dried thyme)
- 1 teaspoon salt
- 1 large onion (chopped)
- 2 large carrots
- 1 cup mushrooms (quartered)
- 1 teaspoon ground black pepper
- ¼ cup fresh parsley

Instructions:
Preheat oven to 300 °F. Preheat olive oil in a Dutch oven over medium-high heat. Add onions, carrots, and mushrooms. Sauté until they start to caramelize, and onions are soft about 9 minutes. Add flour, salt, and pepper. Stir and cook for 120 seconds. Add stock to the pan and stir, working any bits off the bottom of the pot. Add lamb and all remaining ingredients and stir. Cover and bring to a simmer. Once the stew is simmering, transfer pot to the oven and cook for 130 minutes until potatoes are tender. Adjust seasoning, garnish with parsley and serve.

Nutritional Values: Calories: 144 kcal / Carbohydrates: 32 g / Proteins: 24 g / Fiber: 25 g / Fats: 4 g

Beef Stew

Total Time: 5 mins / **Prep. Time:** 5 mins / **Cooking Time:** / **Difficulty:** Easy
Serving Size: 4 servings

Ingredients:

- 2 pounds stewing beef trimmed and cubed
- 4 tablespoons flour
- ½ cup red wine optional
- 2 cups potatoes peeled and cubed
- 4 carrots cut into 1-inch pieces
- 3 stalks celery cut into 1-inch pieces
- 2 tablespoons tomato paste
- 1 teaspoon dried rosemary or 1 sprig fresh
- 3 tablespoons cornstarch
- ¾ cup peas
- ½ teaspoon garlic powder
- 1/3 teaspoon salt
- ½ teaspoon black pepper
- 2 tablespoons olive oil
- 1 onion chopped
- 4 cups beef broth

Instructions:
Combine flour, garlic powder and salt & pepper. Toss beef in flour mixture. Heat olive oil in a large Dutch oven or pot. Cook the beef and onions until browned. Add beef broth and red wine while scraping up any brown bits in the pan. Stir in all remaining ingredients except for peas, cornstarch and water. Reduce heat to medium low, cover and simmer 50-60 minutes or until beef is tender. Mix equal parts cornstarch and water to create a slurry. Slowly add the slurry to the boiling stew to reach desired consistency. Stir in peas and simmer 20 minutes before serving. Season with salt & pepper to taste.

Nutritional Values: Calories: 1122 kcal / Carbohydrates: 18 g / Proteins: 48 g / Fiber: 12 g / Fats: 9 g

Curried Coconut Carrot Soup

Total Time: 45 mins / **Prep. Time:** 10 mins / **Cooking Time:** 35 mins / **Difficulty:** Easy
Serving Size: 5 servings

Ingredients:
- 3 tablespoons coconut oil
- 4 cups vegetable stock
- 1 15-ounce can full-fat coconut milk
- 1 onion, peeled and roughly chopped
- 2 tablespoons freshly chopped ginger root
- 1.5 tablespoon curry powder
- 1/3 teaspoon chili flake
- 6 cups carrots

- Salt and pepper to taste

Instructions:
Heat the coconut oil in a large soup pot and add the onions. Sweat the onions on medium heat for about 10 minutes. Add the carrots and cook for another 3 minutes. Pour in the stock and coconut milk. Add the ginger, curry powder and chili flakes. Put a lid on the pot and cook until the carrots are softened, about 20 minutes. When carrots are soft, carefully blend the soup in batches in a blender or use an immersion hand blender and puree until smooth. Season with salt and pepper and garnish with fresh herbs, and more chili flakes, if desired.

Nutritional Values: Calories: 99 kcal / Carbohydrates: 39 g / Proteins: 14 g / Fiber: 45 g / Fats: 10 g

Hot and Sour Soup

Total Time: 60 mins / **Prep. Time:** 10 mins / **Cooking Time:** 15 mins / **Difficulty:** Easy
Serving Size: 8 servings

Ingredients:
- 5 dried shiitake mushrooms
- 2 tbsp dried black fungus

- For the Pork
- 1/2 tsp Shaoxing wine or water
- 1/2 tsp soy's sauce
- 1/3 tsp cornstarch
- 1/6 cup lean pork, cut into thin strips
- 1/3 tsp white pepper
- For Soup
- 6 cups chicken stock
- 1 tsp white pepper
- 2 Tbs cornstarch
- 1/3 tsp white pepper
- 1/4 tsp sugar
- 1 tsp grated ginger
- ¼ cup carrot, julienne
- ½ cup bamboo shoot, julienne
- 2 eggs, beaten
- 1/3 cup soy sauce
- 1/4 cup white vinegar or Chinese black vinegar
- 1/3 tsp dark soy sauce

- 8 zo silken tofu

- Garnish
- Chopped green onion / cilantro
- Sesame oil

Instructions:
Soak dried mushrooms in warm water for 50 minutes or until soften. Cut into thin strips and set aside. Combine all ingredients for pork and set aside. Bring chicken stock to a boil. While waiting sock to boil, combine soy sauce, vinegar, cornstarch, white pepper and sugar in a mixing bowl until cornstarch and sugar has dissolved. When stock is boiling, add prepared mushrooms, carrot, bamboo shoot and pork. Stir quickly before pork is become a big chunk. Bring back to boil and add soy sauce mixture while stirring soup. Bring back soup to boil once again, pour beaten eggs with a circling motion. Trying to make sure eggs have as many spaces from each other's as possible. Stir as zig zag motion. Immediately add silken tofu and gently stir soup. Be gentle as possible to not to break silken tofu. When soup is start boiling again, it's ready to serve! Enjoy!

Nutritional Values: Calories: 109 kcal / Carbohydrates: 12 g / Proteins: 15 g / Fiber: 18 g / Fats: 14 g

Basil Chicken in Coconut-Curry Sauce

Total Time: 1.5 hours / **Prep. Time:** 10 mins / **Cooking Time:** 20 mins / **Difficulty:** Easy
Serving Size: 8 servings

Ingredients:
- A pinch salt
- 1/4 teaspoon ground coriander
- 1/2 teaspoon ground cumin
- 1 tablespoon cooking oil
- 1 large red onion, chopped
- 3 cloves garlic, minced
- 2 jalapeno peppers, seeded and minced
- 1 13.5 ounce can coconut milk
- 3 teaspoons cornstarch
- 2 tablespoons fresh basil, chopped
- 1 tablespoon finely chopped fresh gingerroot
- 1/3 teaspoon ground cloves

- 1/2 teaspoon ground cinnamon
- 1/4 teaspoon ground cardamon
- 1/3 teaspoon freshly ground black pepper
- 1/3 teaspoon chili powder
- 1/3 teaspoon ground turmeric
- 4 skinless, boneless chicken breasts halves
- Hot cooked rice, for serving

Instructions:
In a small bowl, combine the salt, coriander, cumin, cloves, cinnamon, cardamom, black pepper, chili powder and turmeric. Set aside. Place the chicken pieces into a medium-sized bowl. Sprinkle the spice mixture evenly over the chicken and stir to coat all of the pieces completely. Cover the bowl with plastic wrap and let the chicken stand at room temperature for 45 minutes. In a large skillet, heat the oil over medium-high heat. Add the onion, garlic and jalapeno and cook, stirring constantly, until the onions are soft and translucent 7 minutes. Remove the onion mixture to a clean bowl, reserving the drippings in the skillet. Sautee half the chicken in the skillet for about 4 minutes or until the chicken is tender and no pink remains. Remove the chicken from the pan and place into the bowl with the cooked onion mixture. Repeat with the remaining chicken and once cooked, place into the same bowl. In a bowl, whisk together the coconut milk and cornstarch, and then add it to the skillet. Cook, stirring constantly, until the mixture is thick and bubbly. Add the chicken and onion mixture to the skillet and also add in the basil and gingerroot. Stir to combine and then cook for about 5 minutes or until the mixture is completely heated. Serve immediately over hot cooked rice.

Nutritional Values: Calories: 97 kcal / Carbohydrates: 25 g / Proteins: 42 g / Fiber: 14 g / Fats: 5 g

CHAPTER 16: Fruit smoothies and juices

Asian Slaw

Total Time: 15 mins / **Prep. Time:** 5 mins / **Cooking Time:** 10 mins / **Difficulty:** Easy
Serving Size: 4 servings

Ingredients:
Veggies
- 1.5 cup of snow peas, julienned
- half of red, orange or yellow bell pepper, julienned
- 6 green onions sliced thin on a bias
- 1/3 cup of loosely packed torn cilantro
- 1/3 head of red cabbage, sliced thin (about three cups)
- 1/3 head of savory cabbage (about 2 cups)
- 4 medium size carrots, julienned
- 1/3 cup of loosely packed torn Thai or purple basil

Dressing
- 2 tablespoons vegetable or peanut oil
- 2 teaspoons of soy sauce
- 1/2 teaspoon of brown sugar
- juice of 1 lime
- 1 teaspoon of ginger, minced and smashed to a paste
- 3 teaspoons sesame oil
- 3 tablespoons rice wine vinegar
- 2 cloves of garlic, minced and smashed to a paste

Instructions:
Toss veggies in a large mixing bowl. In a small mixing bowl, add all dressing ingredients and whisk vigorously until well blended. Pour over veggies. Toss. Add salt and pepper to taste and serve.

Nutritional Values: Calories: 94 kcal / Carbohydrates: 32 g / Proteins: 19 g / Fiber: 32 g / Fats: 5 g

Baked Lobster Tail

Total Time: 50 mins / **Prep. Time:** 10 mins / **Cooking Time:** 30 mins / **Difficulty:** Easy
Serving Size: 4 servings

Ingredients:
- 3 teaspoons juice of fresh lemon
- 1/2 cup water
- 1/2 teaspoon salt
- 4 pieces lobster tails 7 oz. each
- 3 tablespoons olive oil
- 3 teaspoons parsley flakes
- A pinch of ground black pepper

Instructions:
Preheat oven to 350 °F. Make a vertical slit on the lobster tail using a pair of kitchen shears. Start from the top part moving towards the tail end. Expose the lobster meat by gently pulling the sides created by the slit in opposite directions. Pull the meat using your hands. Do not completely remove the meat. Arrange the lobster in a baking. Combine salt, pepper, oil, and parsley in a bowl. Using a basting brush, brush the butter mixture over the exposed meat of the lobster. Pour water on the baking tray where the lobster tails are sitting. Bake for 30 minutes. Let cool and then transfer to a serving plate. Serve with lemon butter sauce. Enjoy!

Nutritional Values: Calories: 104 kcal / Carbohydrates: 35 g / Proteins: 14 g / Fiber: 16 g / Fats: 4 g

Pan Seared Ahi Tuna

Total Time: 60 mins / **Prep. Time:** 20 mins / **Cooking Time:** 5 mins / **Difficulty:** Medium
Serving Size: 2 servings

Ingredients:
- 2 ahi tuna steaks, cleaned and patted dry with paper towels
- 4 Tbsp of sesame oil
- 3 Tbsp of the marinade
- Black and white sesame seeds

For the marinade and glaze:
- 1/2 cup water
- some freshly grated ginger
- 2 Tbsp soy sauce
- 1 Tbsp hoisin sauce
- 1/2 tsp of salt
- 1 oz. of brown sugar
- Black pepper
- 1 tsp. of cornstarch mixed with a bit of water

Salad
- Spring mix
- pine nuts
- wasabi paste

For the dressing:

- 1/3 cup of extra virgin olive oil
- 1 Tbsp of apple cider vinegar
- 4 Tbsp lemon juice
- 1 Tbsp orange juice
- 2 of sesame oil
- 1.5 Tbsp of Chinese style hot mustard(optional)
- salt and pepper to taste

Instructions:

Make your marinade using ingredients stated above. Then, take your ahi tuna steaks and toss them in some sesame oil, along with 3 T. of the marinade. Next, gently roll all sides of the ahi tuna steaks in some black and white, toasted sesame seeds. Reserve the rest of the marinade to make the glaze. While the ahi is resting, place the remainder of the marinade in a saucepan, and bring to a quick rolling boil. When it boils, quickly stir in your cornstarch and water mixture. When sauce starts to thicken, turn off and remove from heat. Set aside. Place your cast iron skillet on medium high heat and wait for it to slightly smoke. Carefully add in your tuna steaks and cook on first side for 60 seconds. Flip it over gently using your hand and flat spatula and cook on the other side for 60 more seconds. Flip again and do the sides as well. When the ahi is done, remove from heat, place in wrapped foil, and put it in the freezer for 45 minutes to stop it from cooking. While the ahi is in the freezer, prepare your salad and salad dressing. Remove ahi from freezer and slice to preferred thickness. Plate your salad and tuna and take your thickened sauce from earlier and place in disposable bag. Snip the tip of the disposable bag and drizzle the sauce directly on the ahi. Decorate the plate with more glaze, wasabi paste, and some pine nuts. Serve.

Nutritional Values: Calories: 114 kcal / Carbohydrates: 8 g / Proteins: 38 g / Fiber: 6 g / Fats: 14 g

Easy Perfect Mahi Mahi

Total Time: 30 mins / **Prep. Time:** 10 mins / **Cooking Time:** 15 mins / **Difficulty:** Easy
Serving Size: 4 servings

Ingredients:
- For the Lemon Garlic Mixture:
- 2 TB salted butter, softened to room temp
- 2 TB freshly chopped chives or parsley
- 3 TB garlic cloves, minced

- ⅛ tsp salt
- ¼ tsp freshly ground black pepper
- 1 TB juice from fresh lemon
- 1 TB grated lemon peel

- For the Fish:
- 2 TB olive oil
- 4 1-inch thick each mahi-mahi fillets, 4oz each
- kosher salt and freshly ground black pepper

Instructions:

Preheat oven to 385 °F with rack on middle position. Lemon Garlic Mixture. In a small pan, combine all Lemon Garlic Mixture ingredients and stir to fully combine. Set aside. Pat-dry all excess moisture from the fish fillets with paper towels. Evenly sprinkle both sides of fillets with pinches of salt and freshly ground black pepper. Set aside. In a large oven-proof pan, heat the olive oil over high heat. Once oil is hot adding the fish fillets to pan and let cook until browned on one side, about 2 minutes. Carefully flip fish fillets over to the other side, turn stove burner off, and immediately transfer pan into already-hot oven. Roast fish 10-15 minutes or just until the top is golden and center is just cooked through. Heat your small pan of prepared lemon-garlic mixture over medium high heat, constantly stirring, just until melted and bubbly. Immediately turn heat off and pour mixture over the cooked fish. Be sure to pour on any juices from the fish pan as well. Serve with extra lemon slices for garnish.

Nutritional Values: Calories: 122 kcal / Carbohydrates: 8 g / Proteins: 44 g / Fiber: 10 g / Fats: 17 g

Spicy Carrot Juice

Total Time: 5 mins / **Prep. Time:** 5 mins / **Cooking Time:** / **Difficulty:** Easy
Serving Size: 1 servings

Ingredients:
- 1/3 tsp hot curry powder
- 1 cup carrot juice
- 2 tbsp milk
- 2 small limes
- 1 sprig cilantro
- 1/3 tsp mild curry powder

Instructions:

Squeeze out juice from lime. Rinse the cilantro, shake dry, pluck leaves and cut into fine strips. Mix together mild and hot curry powder in a small bowl. Combine the carrot juice and lime juice with 2/3 of the curry mixture in a tall vessel and puree briefly with an immersion blender. Combine the remaining curry mixture with the milk and blend with a milk frothier to a stiff foam. Pour the carrot juice mixture into a tall serving glass, spoon the curry foam on top, sprinkle with cilantro and serve immediately.

Nutritional Values: Calories: 55 kcal / Carbohydrates: 2 g / Proteins: 1 g / Fiber: 8 g / Fats: 0 g

Immune Boosting Juice

Total Time: 5 mins / **Prep. Time:** 5 mins / **Cooking Time:** / **Difficulty:** Easy
Serving Size: 2 servings

Ingredients:
- 2 cups tomato juice low sodium chilled
- 1 cup baby spinach
- 1/3 cup parsley fresh
- 1/4 teaspoon cloves
- 1/A pinch of pepper
- 1/4 teaspoon turmeric
- 1/8 teaspoon cinnamon

Instructions:
Add all the ingredients to a blender or juicer and blend until smooth.
Nutritional Values: Calories: 68 kcal / Carbohydrates: 1 g / Proteins: 2 g / Fiber: 3 g / Fats: 0 g

Mojito Green Juice

Total Time: 5 mins / **Prep. Time:** 5 mins / **Cooking Time:** / **Difficulty:** Easy
Serving Size: 4 servings

Ingredients:

- 1 lime
- ½ inch fresh ginger
- 2 ½ cucumbers
- 1 small bunch mint
- 1 small bunch parsley
- 1 green apple

Instructions:
Push mint, parsley, lime, ginger, cucumbers, and apple through a juicer. Serve

Nutritional Values: Calories: 50 kcal / Carbohydrates: 2 g / Proteins: 1 g / Fiber: 4 g / Fats: 0 g

Delicious Kale Smoothie

Total Time: 5 mins / **Prep. Time:** 5 mins / **Cooking Time:** / **Difficulty:** Easy
Serving Size: 4 servings

Ingredients:
- 1 cup kale
- 1 banana
- 1 tablespoon unsweetened peanut butter
- 1 tablespoon maple syrup or any other sweetener of your choice
- 1 tablespoon lemon juice
- 1 cup unsweetened almond milk or any other nut milk
- water or ice optional
- a pinch of sea salt

Instructions:
Blend all the ingredients in a blender until smooth. Add a bit of ice or water to adjust the consistency and a pinch of salt to balance the taste. Enjoy!

Nutritional Values: Calories: 85 kcal / Carbohydrates: 4 g / Proteins: 3 g / Fiber: 4 g / Fats: 6 g

Aam Ka Panna Spiced Green Mango Juice

Total Time: 5 mins / **Prep. Time:** 5 mins / **Cooking Time:** / **Difficulty:** Easy
Serving Size: 2 servings

Ingredients:
- 1 med-large Green mango, washed

- few ice cubes
- About 2 cups cold water
- 3 tsp roasted Cumin Powder
- 1 tsp Black Salt
- 1/3 tsp ground Black Pepper
- 2 tbsp Sugar, to taste
- few Mint leaves to garnish

Instructions:
The amount of spices depend largely on how tangy/sour the Mango is. It will also vary on your taste preferences. The idea is creating a flavor where you get the sweet and sour balance from the mango and sugar along with the heat of the spices. The amount of sugar will depend on the sourness of the mangoes. The firmer the mangoes, sourer it probably will be. Some people tend to use little ripe mango which will be little sweeter than the unripe ones, you will need to add less sugar.

Nutritional Values: Calories: 90 kcal / Carbohydrates: 3 g / Proteins: 1 g / Fiber: 10 g / Fats: 2 g

Aam Ka Panna Spiced Green Mango Juice

Total Time: 5 mins / **Prep. Time:** 5 mins / **Cooking Time:** / **Difficulty:** Easy
Serving Size: 2 servings

Ingredients:
- 1 med-large Green mango, washed
- few ice cubes
- About 2 cups cold water
- 3 tsp roasted Cumin Powder
- 1 tsp Black Salt
- 1/3 tsp ground Black Pepper
- 2 tbsp Sugar, to taste
- few Mint leaves to garnish

Instructions:
The amount of spices depend largely on how tangy/sour the Mango is. It will also vary on your taste preferences. The idea is creating a flavor where you get the sweet and sour balance from the mango and sugar along with the heat of the spices. The amount of sugar will depend on the sourness of the mangoes. The firmer the mangoes, sourer it probably will be. Some people tend to use little ripe

mango which will be little sweeter than the unripe ones, you will need to add less sugar.

Nutritional Values: Calories: 90 kcal / Carbohydrates: 3 g / Proteins: 1 g / Fiber: 10 g / Fats: 2 g

Anti-Inflammatory Turmeric Latte

Total Time: 5 mins / **Prep. Time:** 5 mins / **Cooking Time:** / **Difficulty:** Easy
Serving Size: 4 servings

Ingredients:
- 1/3 tsp coconut oil
- pinch of black pepper
- 1 cup unsweetened almond milk or non-dairy milk of choice
- 1/3 tsp ginger juice squeezed from grated ginger root
- 1/3 tsp vanilla extract
- 1/3 tsp ground turmeric powder
- 1/4 tsp cinnamon
- 1/3 tsp maple syrup

Instructions:
Melt the coconut oil in a small saucepan over medium heat. Add the turmeric, cinnamon and black pepper, and stir them around in the coconut oil for about 30s.

Nutritional Values: Calories: 100 kcal / Carbohydrates: 6 g / Proteins: 8 g / Fiber: 8 g / Fats: 3 g

Healthy Juice

Total Time: 5 mins / **Prep. Time:** 5 mins / **Cooking Time:** / **Difficulty:** Easy
Serving Size: 4 servings

Ingredients:
- 1 cup freshly squeezed orange juice
- 1 cup kale
- 3 inches ginger root
- 1 lemon, squeezed for juice
- 2 cups organic raspberries
- ½ pound mango, chopped
- 1 cup young Thai coconut water

Instructions:
Put all of the ingredients into a blender and pulse blend for 15-20 seconds to best minimize oxidation.

Serve

Nutritional Values: Calories: 72 kcal / Carbohydrates: 3 g / Proteins: 4 g / Fiber: 12 g / Fats: 0 g

Citrus Berry Smoothie

Total Time: 5 mins / **Prep. Time:** 5 mins / **Cooking Time:** / **Difficulty:** Easy
Serving Size: 4 servings

Ingredients:
- 1/3 cup orange juice
- 3 tablespoons milk
- 1 tablespoon wheat germ
- 1 1/2 cups berries
- 1 cup yogurt (low-fat plain)
- 2 tablespoon honey
- 1/3 teaspoon vanilla extract

Instructions:
Place berries, yogurt, orange juice, dry milk, wheat germ, honey and vanilla in a blender and blend until smooth.

Nutritional Values: Calories: 66 kcal / Carbohydrates: 2 g / Proteins: 4 g / Fiber: 6 g / Fats: 1 g

Pineapple Ginger Juice

Total Time: 5 mins / **Prep. Time:** 5 mins / **Cooking Time:** / **Difficulty:** Easy
Serving Size: 2-7 servings

Ingredients:
- ½ cup ginger chopped
- 1-2 cups fresh pineapple juice
- 2 cups water
- 1 cup granulated sugar
- Hot water 4 pounds
- Juice of freshly squeezed lime

Instructions:
In a large bowl, mix ginger and hot water. Let it sit for about an hour or more. Using a cheesecloth or fine sieve, drain the water and set aside. In a medium bowl bring to a boil 2 cups water and sugar. Simmer until sugar has dissolved. Allow to cool. Combine ginger water, juice and simple syrup stir and serve over ice.

Nutritional Values: Calories: 66 kcal / Carbohydrates: 5 g / Proteins: 5 g / Fiber: 9 g / Fats: 0 g

Green Monster

Total Time: 5 mins / **Prep. Time:** 5 mins / **Cooking Time:** / **Difficulty:** Easy
Serving Size: 3 servings

Ingredients:
- 1 ½ cup ice cubes
- ½ pound mango frozen
- 1 cup spinach
- 1 cup kale
- 1/2 banana
- 1 apple cored and quartered
- 1 ½ cup orange juice

Instructions
Put all ingredients in a blender and mix for 25 seconds. Stir and mix for 10 more seconds. Serve

Nutritional Values: Calories: 64 kcal / Carbohydrates: 2 g / Proteins: 12 g / Fiber: 10 g / Fats: 0 g

Orange Sunrise

Total Time: 5 mins / Prep. Time: 5 mins / Cooking Time: / Difficulty: Easy
Serving Size: 4 servings

Ingredients:
- 2 orange bell peppers, seeded
- 1 naval orange, peeled
- 6 carrots
- 1 large handful of fresh pineapple chunks
- 1 ½ lemon, peeled

Instructions:
Wash all produce well. Add all ingredients through juicer. Pour over ice and enjoy!

Nutritional Values: Calories: 820 kcal / Carbohydrates: 8 g / Proteins: 7 g / Fiber: 14 g / Fats: 0 g

CHAPTER 17: Dessert

Kiwi Muffins

Total Time: 60 mins / **Prep. Time:** 10 mins / **Cooking Time:** 40 mins / **Difficulty:** Easy
Serving Size: 6 servings

Ingredients:
- 3 tbsp baking powder
- 1 tsp salt
- ½ pound granulated sugar
- 1/2 tsp cinnamon
- 2 egg slightly beaten
- 2 cups milk
- 3 tsp vanilla extract
- 4 kiwi peeled and diced to 1/2" size
- 3 ¾ cups all-purpose flour
- 1/3 cup canola oil
- turbinado sugar for dusting

Instructions:
Preheat oven to 390 °F. Line muffin tins with paper cupcake liners. Sift flour, salt, sugar, cinnamon & baking power in a bowl and mix well. Beat together egg, milk, oil & vanilla in a large bowl. Slowly mix in the dry ingredients. Fold in the chopped kiwi. Spoon mixture into a cupcake liner & fill them to the top. Sprinkle with the raw/turbinado sugar. Bake for 35-40 minutes. Muffins are done when slightly brown & a toothpick inserted into the center comes out clean.

Nutritional Values: Calories: 144 kcal / Carbohydrates: 40 g / Proteins: 24 g / Fiber: 3 g / Fats: 6 g

Strawberry Lemonade

Total Time: 5 mins / **Prep. Time:** 5 mins / **Cooking Time:** / **Difficulty:** Easy
Serving Size: 5 servings

Ingredients:
- Juice of 4 lemons (about 3/4-1 cup of juice)
- Cold water
- Ice (optional)
- 2 cups strawberries cut into halves & tops removed
- ½ pound granulated sugar
- Strawberry and lemon slices for garnish (optional)

Instructions:
Add them to a blender, along with the sugar and enough water so it blends easily. Blend until smooth for 25 seconds. Juice your lemons. Using a sieve, strain the strawberry juice and lemon juice. Transfer the pulp-free strawberry/lemon juice mix to a pitcher. Top up the pitcher with water. Chill or serve right away. If desired, add ice and fruit pieces just prior to serving.

Nutritional Values: Calories: 88 kcal / Carbohydrates: 6 g / Proteins: 3 g / Fiber: 4 g / Fats: 0 g

Mango Shake

Total Time: 5 mins / **Prep. Time:** 5 mins / **Cooking Time:** / **Difficulty:** Easy
Serving Size: 2 servings

Ingredients:
- 4 pieces ripe mango, peeled and sliced
- 1 pound ice cubes
- ½ pound evaporated milk (optional)
- sugar or other sweetener to taste

Instructions:
In a blender, process mango, milk, sugar and some ice until blended. Add more ice until smooth then pour into glasses then served cold.

Nutritional Values: Calories: 100 kcal / Carbohydrates: 38 g / Proteins: 4 g / Fiber: 4 g / Fats: 4 g

Summer Breezes Smoothie

Total Time: 30 mins / **Prep. Time:** 5 mins / **Cooking Time:** / **Difficulty:** Easy
Serving Size: 4 servings

Ingredients:
- 1 cup fresh raspberries
- 1 cup fresh blueberries
- 1 just-ripe medium banana, broken into pieces
- ½ cup natural plain yoghurt
- 1 cup fresh blackberries
- ½ cup milk
- 1 tbsp icing sugar (optional)

Instructions:
Measure all the ingredients into a food processor and whiz until smooth. Alternatively use a hand-held blender. Pour into a tall cool glass and enjoy.

Nutritional Values: Calories: 80 kcal / Carbohydrates: 15 g / Proteins: 3 g / Fiber: 11 g / Fats: 0 g

Microwave Chocolate Pudding

Total Time: 15 mins / **Prep. Time:** 5 mins / **Cooking Time:** 5 mins / **Difficulty:** Easy **Serving Size:** 1 servings

Ingredients:
- ¼ cup baking cocoa
- 3 tablespoons cornstarch
- A pinch salt
- 1 pound cups milk
- 1/3 cup sugar
- 1 teaspoons vanilla
- 1/2 cup chocolate chips

Instructions:
Combine sugar, baking cocoa, cornstarch, and salt in a 1 qt or 2 qt microwave-safe bowl. Whisk in milk until smooth. Microwave on high, uncovered, for 3 minutes. Stir and microwave for 5 more minutes. The time may vary with the different microwave ovens. Stir in vanilla and chocolate chips. Stir until chocolate chips are melted and pudding is smooth. Serve immediately or cool to serve. To avoid the skin that forms on the pudding as it cools, use plastic wrap to cover the pudding and press it directly onto the putting so that it touches the pudding.

Nutritional Values: Calories: 110 kcal / Carbohydrates: 48 g / Proteins: 24 g / Fiber: 2 g / Fats: 10 g

Chocolate Chip Cookies

Total Time: 30 mins / **Prep. Time:** 15 mins / **Cooking Time:** 10 mins/ **Difficulty:** Medium **Serving Size:** 5 servings

Ingredients:
- ¾ cup old-fashioned rolled oats, ground in a food processor or blender until very fine
- 1 cup semi-sweet chocolate chips
- ½ cup loosely packed sweetened flaked coconut
- ¾ cup pecans, chopped
- 1 cup all-purpose flour,
- 1/3 teaspoon baking powder
- ½ teaspoon baking soda
- A pinch salt

- ½ cup unsalted butter, softened but still cool
- 1/3 cup light brown sugar, packed
- ½ cup granulated sugar
- 1 large egg
- 1 teaspoon vanilla

Instructions:
Adjust racks to upper- and lower- middle positions and preheat the oven to 300 °F. Line two cookie sheets with parchment paper and set aside. In a medium bowl, whisk together the ground oats, flour, baking powder, baking soda and salt. In the bowl of an electric mixer, beat the butter and sugars at medium speed until light and fluffy, about 2 minutes. Scrape down the sides of the bowl with a rubber spatula. Add the egg and vanilla; continue beating until combined. Add the dry ingredients and beat at low speed until just combined. Add the chocolate chips, coconut and nuts and mix until evenly combined. Working with 1½ tablespoons of cookie dough at a time, form balls and place on parchment-lined cookie sheets, leaving at least 2 inches between them. Bake, reversing position of cookie sheets halfway through baking, until edges of cookies begin to crisp but centers are still soft. Cool cookies on baking sheets for 60 seconds, then transfer to racks to cool completely. Repeat with remaining batter. Bake as needed directly from the freezer. **Serve**

Nutritional Values: Calories: 144 kcal / Carbohydrates: 38 g / Proteins: 22 g / Fiber: 3 g / Fats: 9 g

Date Honey Nut Cake

Total Time: 5 mins / **Prep. Time:** 5 mins / **Cooking Time:** / **Difficulty:** Easy **Serving Size:** 4 servings

Ingredients:
- ¾ cup whole dates
- 1/4 cup honey
- 2 large eggs
- 1 teaspoon vanilla
- 1/2 cup chopped walnuts
- 1/2 pound cake flour
- 1 teaspoon baking powder
- 1 teaspoon cinnamon
- Pinch salt

- Pinch nutmeg
- 3/4 cup canola oil
- 1/3 cup brown sugar
- Nonstick cooking spray

Instructions:
Preheat oven to 300 °F. Place dates into a bowl and cover them with very hot water. Let the dates soak while you prepare the cake batter. In a large mixing bowl, sift together cake flour, baking powder, cinnamon, salt, and nutmeg. In a medium mixing bowl, whisk together vegetable oil, brown sugar, honey, eggs, and vanilla. Pour the wet ingredients into the dry ingredients and stir till a thick batter forms. Drain water from the dates. Pit the dates, then chop the fruit into small chunks. Fold the walnuts and date chunks into the batter. Generously grease your loaf pan with cooking spray. Pour batter into loaf pan. Place loaf pan in preheated oven. Bake cake for about 90 minutes, or until a toothpick inserted in the center comes out clean. Remove from oven and set on a wire rack to cool.

Nutritional Values: Calories: 116 kcal / Carbohydrates: 46 g / Proteins: 18 g / Fiber: 14 g / Fats: 6 g

Summer Strawberry Shortcake

Total Time: 5 mins / **Prep. Time:** 5 mins / **Cooking Time:** / **Difficulty:** Easy
Serving Size: 4 servings

Ingredients:
- 1-pound all-purpose flour;
- 3 tablespoons granulated sugar;
- 3 teaspoons baking powder;
- 1/3 teaspoon salt;
- 1-pint fresh strawberries, hulled and quartered;
- 1/4 cup granulated sugar;
- 1/2 cup unsalted butter, chilled and cut into small pieces;
- 2/3 cup heavy cream

Instructions:
In a medium bowl, toss together the strawberries and 1/4 cup granulated sugar. Set aside. In a large mixing bowl, whisk together the flour, 2 tablespoons granulated sugar, baking powder, and salt. Using a pastry cutter or your fingers, cut in the butter until the mixture resembles coarse crumbs. Stir in the cream until the dough comes together. Turn the dough out onto a lightly floured surface

and knead gently a few times until it comes together. Pat the dough out into a 1-inch-thick circle. Using a biscuit cutter or a glass, cut out circles of dough. Place the dough circles on a baking sheet lined with parchment paper and brush with a little cream. Bake at 390 °F for 20 minutes, or until golden brown. To assemble, split the shortcakes in half horizontally and top each bottom half with a spoonful of the strawberry mixture. Replace the top half of the shortcake and top with more strawberries and whipped cream. Enjoy!

Nutritional Values: Calories: 102 kcal / Carbohydrates: 12 g / Proteins: 3 g / Fiber: 8 g / Fats: 6 g

Simple Pumpkin Spice Smoothie

Total Time: 5 mins / **Prep. Time:** 5 mins / **Cooking Time:** / **Difficulty:** Easy
Serving Size: 3 servings

Ingredients:
- ¾ pound unsweetened almond milk
- 1 cup fresh, roasted pumpkin puree
- 1/3 cup spinach
- 1.5 teaspoon vanilla extract
- 1/2 teaspoon no sugar pumpkin spice
- 1 tbsp chia seeds
- optional: pumpkin seeds

Instructions:
Blend all ingredients in a high-speed blender. Sprinkle with pumpkin seeds. Enjoy!

Nutritional Values: Calories: 78 kcal / Carbohydrates: 9 g / Proteins: 4 g / Fiber: 14 g / Fats: 2 g

Easy Morning Glory Muffins

Total Time: 60 mins / **Prep. Time:** 10 mins / **Cooking Time:** 40 mins / **Difficulty:** Medium
Serving Size: 5 servings

Ingredients:
- 1-pound oats, gluten-free if needed
- 1/2 cup coconut palm sugar
- 3 tsp vanilla extract
- 1 1/2 tsp ground cinnamon
- 1/2 tsp ground ginger
- 1 medium-sized ripe banana
- 1 cup carrots, shredded

- 1/2 cup apple, shredded
- 2 tsp baking powder
- 1/3 tsp baking soda
- A pinch salt
- ¼ pound unsweetened almond milk
- 1/4 cup almond butter
- 1/3 cup raisins
- 2 oz. walnuts, chopped

Instructions:
Preheat your oven to 300 °F and prepare a muffin pan by lining the cavities with parchment paper liners or greasing them with oil. Set aside. Add the oats, baking powder, baking soda, and salt to a high-speed blender and process on high until the oats have broken down into the consistency of a fine flour, about 15 seconds. Add all of the remaining ingredients except for the carrots, apple, raisins, and walnuts and process on high until the batter becomes smooth and creamy, about 10 seconds. Periodically stop and scrape down the sides/corners of your blender as necessary. Finally, use a spatula to mix in the carrots, apple, raisins, and nuts by hand. Spoon the batter into the prepared muffin cups, filling each one about 3/4 of the way full. Bake for 35-40 minutes, until the tops of the muffins begin to turn golden brown, and a toothpick inserted into the center comes out clean. Allow the muffins to cool in the pan for 10 minutes before transferring them to a wire rack to cool completely. As soon as they've cooled, transfer them to an airtight container and store them at room temperature for up to 3 days, or freeze for up to 2 months.

Nutritional Values: Calories: 114 kcal / Carbohydrates: 21 g / Proteins: 14 g / Fiber: 6 g / Fats: 8 g

Homemade Hot Chocolate Mix

Total Time: 15 mins / **Prep. Time:** 10 mins / **Cooking Time:** / **Difficulty:** Easy
Serving Size: 3 servings

Ingredients:
- 1 cup powdered sugar
- ½ cups cocoa powder
- 1 cup finely chopped white chocolate
- 1.5 pound dry nonfat or whole milk powder

- ¼ teaspoon salt

Instructions:
Whisk together all ingredients in a large bowl. Working in two batches, depending on the size of your food processor, pulse the ingredients in a food processor until the chocolate is finely ground. Store the dry mix in an airtight container for up to 2 months. To make hot cocoa, put 1/3 cup of the cocoa mix in a mug and stir in 1 cup of hot milk or almond milk. Top with whipped cream or miniature marshmallows, if desired.

Nutritional Values: Calories: 133 kcal / Carbohydrates: 42 g / Proteins: 22 g / Fiber: 2 g / Fats: 10 g

Moist Pumpkin Cake

Total Time: 2 hours / **Prep. Time:** 15 mins / **Cooking Time:** 85 mins / **Difficulty:** Easy
Serving Size: 7 servings

Ingredients:
- 1 cup granulated sugar
- 3/4 cup light brown sugar
- 1 teaspoon cinnamon
- 1.5 teaspoon pumpkin spice
- ½ teaspoon nutmeg
- 1/3 teaspoon salt
- 2 cups Pumpkin
- Cinnamon & Sugar Cake Coating
- ¼ cup granulated sugar
- 1 cup canola oil can also use vegetable oil
- 3 teaspoons baking soda
- 3 large eggs room temperature
- 2 ¾ cups all-purpose flour
- ½ tablespoon cinnamon

Instructions:
Make sure the oven rack is adjusted to the center position. Preheat the oven to 300 °F. Spray a 10-cup Bundt pan with nonstick spray. In a large bowl, combine the oil and sugars until fluffy; add eggs one at a time. In another bowl, combine the flour, baking soda, cinnamon, pumpkin spice, nutmeg, salt. Add the pumpkin and dry mixture to the fluffy sugar mixture alternating between both to make sure everything is well-combined. Add mixture to the greased Bundt pan. Bake for 70-85 minutes or until a toothpick inserted into the center of the cake comes out clean. This cake will be a deep brown, and spring back when gently pressed. Allow this cake to fully cool for at least one hour before transferring it

to a wire rack. Once transferred, sprinkle cinnamon and sugar around the cake over the sink to keep things clean. Transfer your cake carefully to a cake stand or platter.

Nutritional Values: Calories: 100 kcal / Carbohydrates: 39 g / Proteins: 14 g / Fiber: 4 g / Fats: 9 g

Strawberry granita

Total Time: 5 hours / **Prep. Time:** 1 hour / **Cooking Time:** / **Difficulty:** Easy
Serving Size: 4 servings

Ingredients:
- 1/3 cup chopped fresh mint leaves
- 1 ¾ cups chopped strawberries
- 1/3 cup coconut milk
- 1 cup water
- 1/4 cup honey
- 2 tbsp lemon juice
- pinch salt

Instructions:
In a small saucepan, combine water, 1/4 cup honey and mint leaves. Simmer on low while you prepare the strawberry mixture. Pour the strawberries into a food processor and add the honey and puree. Add the coconut milk, lemon juice and salt and process again until well-combined. Strain the mint leaves out of the water mixture and pour the water mixture into the strawberries. Process again, then pour into a glass dish, 8×8 or 9×9 and place in freezer for 5 hours, until frozen. To serve, scrape with a fork and scoop out. This will help ensure a "fluffy" texture.

Nutritional Values: Calories: 94 kcal / Carbohydrates: 3 g / Proteins: 0 g / Fiber: 4 g / Fats: 2 g

Warm Apple Crisp

Total Time: 1.5 hours / **Prep. Time:** 10 mins / **Cooking Time:** 55 mins / **Difficulty:** Easy
Serving Size: 4 servings

Ingredients:

- 6 apples, cored and chopped
- 3 teaspoons lemon juice
- 1 teaspoon vanilla extract
- 1/3 cup rolled oats
- 1/4 cup coconut sugar
- 1/4 teaspoon ground cinnamon
- 1/4 cup grass-fed butter, softened to room temperature

Instructions:
Preheat the oven to 355 °F. In a medium bowl, combine the apples, lemon juice, and vanilla. Spread the apple mixture evenly in a medium baking dish. Combine the oats, sugar, and cinnamon in a bowl. Cut the butter into the mixture with your fingers, until it forms a crumbly consistency. Sprinkle the oat mixture evenly over the apple mixture. Bake for 55 minutes or until the apples are tender and the topping is golden brown. Serve warm.

Nutritional Values: Calories: 85 kcal / Carbohydrates: 28 g / Proteins: 8 g / Fiber: 12 g / Fats: 0 g

Grilled Peaches With Cinnamon and Brown Sugar

Total Time: 20 mins / **Prep. Time:** 10 mins / **Cooking Time:** 10 mins / **Difficulty:** Easy
Serving Size: 3 servings

Ingredients:
- 2 tablespoons packed light brown sugar
- ½ tablespoon ground cinnamon
- 3 peaches, halved and pits removed
- 1 tablespoon unsalted butter, melted

Instructions:
Preheat grill to medium heat. Mix brown sugar and cinnamon in a small bowl. Set aside. Lightly brush the cut side of peaches with melted butter. Place peaches, cut side down, onto grill pan. Grill for about 2 minutes, or until peaches start to soften just a little and grill marks form. Flip peaches over and sprinkle tops with cinnamon brown sugar mixture. Grill for an additional 4 minutes, or until sugar mixture begins to caramelize. Remove peaches from grill pan. Serve immediately with yogurt or ice cream, if desired.

Nutritional Values: Calories: 94 kcal / Carbohydrates: 24 g / Proteins: 3 g / Fiber: 14 g / Fats: 1 g

Energy Bites

Total Time: 45 mins / **Prep. Time:** 10 mins / **Cooking Time:** / **Difficulty:** Easy
Serving Size: 4 servings

Ingredients:
- 1 cup quick cooking rolled oats
- ½ cup mini chocolate chips
- ¼ cup protein powder
- ½ cup all-natural peanut butter
- ⅓ cup honey
- ½ pound shredded coconut
- ½ cup milled flaxseed
- 1 teaspoon vanilla extract

Instructions:
In a large bowl, combine oats, coconut, flaxseed, chocolate chips and protein powder and mix together. Add peanut butter, honey and vanilla and mix well. Refrigerate for 30 minutes. Once chilled, use a small cookie scoop to scoop out mixture and use your hands to help roll it into small, bite-sized balls. Store in an airtight container in the refrigerator fridge. Separate the layers with parchment or wax paper.

Nutritional Values: Calories: 110 kcal / Carbohydrates: 42 g / Proteins: 16 g / Fiber: 5 g / Fats: 8 g

Mini Pecan Phyllo Tarts

Total Time: 35 mins / **Prep. Time:** 10 mins / **Cooking Time:** 25 mins / **Difficulty:** Easy
Serving Size: 3 servings

Ingredients:
- 1 tbsp butter, melted
- 1/3 tsp vanilla
- 1/2 cup pecans chopped
- 1 large egg
- 3 tsp brown sugar
- 3 tbsp honey
- 15 dry and flat biscuits (like Mini Phyllo Shells, Athens)

Instructions:
Preheat oven to 300°F. In a medium mixing bowl, combine all ingredients except pecans. Mix well. Stir in chopped pecans. Arrange mini shells on a baking sheet. Fill mini shells with one heaping teaspoon of pecan mixture. If any of the mixture remains, distribute evenly between all the shells.

Bake for 20-25 minutes. Let them cool before serving.

Nutritional Values: Calories: 100 kcal / Carbohydrates: 16 g / Proteins: 12 g / Fiber: 1 g / Fats: 4 g

Healthy Chocolate Cake

Total Time: 50 mins / **Prep. Time:** 10 mins / **Cooking Time:** 30 mins / **Difficulty:** Medium
Serving Size: 4 servings

Ingredients:
- 1/3 tsp salt
- 3/4 cup granulated sugar of choice or xylitol
- 1/2 cup mini chocolate chips, optional
- 1/4 cup yogurt
- 1 cup spelt, white, or gf ap flour
- 3 oz cocoa powder
- 1/3 tsp baking soda
- 1 cup water
- 1/4 cup almond butter
- 3 tsp pure vanilla extract

Instructions:
Preheat oven to 330 °F and grease an 8-in square or round pan. Set aside. In a large bowl, combine the flour, cocoa powder, baking soda, salt, optional chips, and sweetener, and stir very well. In a new bowl, whisk together the nut butter, yogurt, water, and vanilla. Pour wet into dry and stir until just combined (don't over-mix), then pour into the greased pan. Bake 30 minutes or until batter has risen and a toothpick inserted into the center of the cake comes out mostly clean. Serve

Nutritional Values: Calories: 100 kcal / Carbohydrates: 10 g / Proteins: 3 g / Fiber: 1 g / Fats: 9 g

Key Lime Cream Cheese Frosted Cake Doughnut

Total Time: 40 mins / **Prep. Time:** 10 mins / **Cooking Time:** 25 mins / **Difficulty:** Easy
Serving Size: 4 servings

Ingredients:
For The Donuts:

- 1 cup all-purpose flour
- 2 Tbs. + 2 tsp. grapeseed oil
- 1/4 cup + 2 Tbs. sugar
- 1/3 cup + 2 Tbs. milk
- 1 tsp. baking powder
- 1/3 tsp. kosher salt
- 1/3 tsp. key lime zest
- 1/2 tsp. vanilla
- 1 egg

For The Frosting:
- 2 ounces cream cheese, room temperature
- 3-4 Tbs. powdered sugar
- 1 Tbs. heavy cream
- 1 Tbs. key lime juice (more or less to taste)
- 1/2 tsp. vanilla
- Additional lime zest or sprinkles for garnish, if desired

Instructions:
Preheat oven to 300 °F. Spray or grease a 6-cavity doughnut pan. Combine flour, baking powder, salt and lime zest in a small bowl. Whisk to blend and set aside. In a medium bowl, whisk oil, sugar, milk, vanilla and egg until well-combined. Add dry ingredients to the wet ingredients and stir until well-blended. Spoon into doughnut pan and bake for 25 minutes until the donuts bounce back when lightly touched. Remove from pan and let cool on a wire rack. While the donuts are cooling, whisk the cream cheese, 2 tablespoons powdered sugar, heavy cream, lime juice and vanilla in a wide, shallow bowl. If the frosting is too thin, add another tablespoon of powdered sugar. When the doughnuts are mostly cool, dip the tops in the frosting, and return them to the wire rack to let the frosting set. Repeat with the other doughnuts.

Nutritional Values: Calories: 150 kcal / Carbohydrates: 42 g / Proteins: 16 g / Fiber: 4 g / Fats: 13 g

Rainbow Fruit Salad

Total Time: 5 mins / **Prep. Time:** 5 mins / **Cooking Time:** / **Difficulty:** Easy
Serving Size: 4 servings

Ingredients:
Fruit salad:

- 2 cups fresh blueberries
- 2 bananas, sliced
- 1-pound fresh strawberries, halved
- 1 large mango, peeled and diced
- 1-pound seedless grapes
- 2 nectarines, unpeeled and sliced
- 1 kiwi fruit, peeled and sliced

Honey orange sauce:
- 1/2 cup unsweetened orange juice
- 3 tablespoons lemon juice
- 2 tablespoons honey
- 1/4 teaspoon ground ginger
- dash nutmeg

Instructions:
Combine all the ingredients for the sauce and mix. Just before serving, pour honey orange sauce over the fruit.

Nutritional Values: Calories: 82 kcal / Carbohydrates: 8 g / Proteins: 4 g / Fiber: 6 g / Fats: 9 g

Flourless Banana Bread

Total Time: 5 mins / **Prep. Time:** 5 mins / **Cooking Time:** / **Difficulty:** Easy
Serving Size: 4 servings

Ingredients:
- 3 medium ripe bananas
- 2 large eggs
- 1/3 cup pure maple syrup
- 1 teaspoon baking soda
- 1 pound old-fashioned rolled oats

Instructions:
Preheat oven to 330 °F. Lightly grease 9×5-inch loaf pan with non-stick cooking spray and set aside. Add all ingredients to a blender, in the order listed, and blend until smooth and well combined. Pour batter into prepared loaf pan. Bake for 40-45 minutes or until a toothpick inserted in the center comes out clean. Let loaf cool completely in loaf pan. Store bread in an airtight container on the counter for 2-3 days or in the refrigerator for up to a week.

Nutritional Values: Calories: 92 kcal / Carbohydrates: 38 g / Proteins: 12 g / Fiber: 10 g / Fats: 13 g

Whole Orange Almond Cake

Total Time: 3 hours / **Prep. Time:** 25 mins / **Cooking Time:** 2.5 hours / **Difficulty:** Easy **Serving Size:** 4 servings

Ingredients:
- 2 Organic Navel Oranges
- ½ pound Egg Whites
- ½ tsp Almond Flavor
- 2 cups Almond Flour
- ¾ cup Oat Flour
- 1 cup Granulated Erythritol
- 2 tsp Double-Acting Baking Powder

Instructions:
Wash the oranges thoroughly then pierce all over with a knife. Place the oranges in a large pot and cover with water. Bring this to a full boil, then lower the heat to medium/low-low and cover. Simmer for 50-60 minutes, drain and let cool slightly. Cut the oranges into quarters, discard all seeds and puree in a blender. Preheat the oven to 300 °F and spray an 8" cake pan with cooking spray. In a medium-sized bowl, whisk together the almond flour, oat flour, erythritol and baking powder. In a large bowl, add the orange puree, egg whites and almond flavor. Whisk well. Dump the dry ingredients over the wet and fold together. Make sure there are no clumps. Pour batter into prepared pan and bake for 90 minutes, or until surface of cake springs back when touched. Cool cake in pan for about 30 minutes, then flip onto a wire cooling rack, leaving pan over top for another 40 minutes. Remove pan and let cool completely. Slice and serve!

Nutritional Values: Calories: 110 kcal / Carbohydrates: 45 g / Proteins: 15 g / Fiber: 4 g / Fats: 8 g

Rich Chocolate Cake

Total Time: 60 mins / **Prep. Time:** 10 mins / **Cooking Time:** 45 mins / **Difficulty:** Easy **Serving Size:** 4 servings

Ingredients:

- 1 cup dark chocolate
- 3 large eggs
- 3 tablespoons chocolate powder
- 1 teaspoon baking powder
- 4 oz. teaspoon baking soda
- 9 oz. unsalted butter
- 1 ¾ sugar
- 1 cup cake flour, sifted
- 8 oz. fresh full milk

Ganache Topping:
- 7 oz. dark chocolate
- 4 oz. heavy whipping cream
- 3-4 tbsp unsalted butter

Other Optional Toppings:
- Strawberries
- Powdered sugar

Instructions:
Melt the dark chocolate in a double boiler. Set aside to cool. Beat the butter and sugar until light and fluffy. Add in the eggs, one at a time, beating well after each addition. Pour in the melted chocolate, chocolate powder, baking powder and baking soda. Fold in the cake flour in 3 batches, alternate with the fresh milk. Pour the batter into an 8-inch rectangle cake pan or round cake pan. Bake at a pre-heated oven at 330 °F for about 40-45 minutes. Test with a cake tester, make sure it comes out clean. Remove the Chocolate Cake and let cool

Nutritional Values: Calories: 132 kcal / Carbohydrates: 45 g / Proteins: 22 g / Fiber: 4 g / Fats: 4 g

Simple cake

Total Time: 1.5 hours / **Prep. Time:** 15 mins / **Cooking Time:** 45 mins / **Difficulty:** Easy **Serving Size:** 4 servings

Ingredients:
- 4 medium eggs
- ½ cup granulated sugar
- 1 ¾ cup all-purpose flour
- 1.5 teaspoon baking powder
- 4 oz. melted unsalted butter
- Juice of one lemon
- Zest of one lemon

Instructions:
Preheat the oven to 300 °F. Grease a Bundt cake pan (24 x 8 centimeters) with margarine and dust with some flour. In an electric mixer, beat on medium speed the sugar, eggs and the lemon zest until obtain a homogeneous mixture. Add the melted

butter, lemon juice and mix for 90 seconds until it's nicely incorporated. Add the flour and the baking powder and beat until a creamy mixture. Pour the mixture into the prepared pan and bake until a toothpick inserted in the center comes out clean, about 45 minutes (the time depends on the oven). When the cake is cooked, remove from the oven and unmold onto a plate. Let cool to room temperature and serve.

Nutritional Values: Calories: 108 kcal / Carbohydrates: 38 g / Proteins: 22 g / Fiber: 7 g / Fats: 10 g

Cinnamon Sugar Apple Cake

Total Time: 90 mins / **Prep. Time:** 20 mins / **Cooking Time:** 60 minutes / **Difficulty:** Easy
Serving Size: 6 servings

Ingredients:
- 1 1/3 cups brown sugar
- 1.5 teaspoon baking soda
- 1 egg
- 1 cup buttermilk
- 4 oz. sugar
- 1 teaspoon cinnamon
- 1 teaspoon vanilla extract
- 1-pound all-purpose flour
- 1 1/2 cups chopped apples
- 1/2 cup canola oil
- 1 tablespoon melted butter

Instructions:
Preheat oven to 300 °F and grease a 9×13-inch pan with cooking spray. In a large bowl, whisk together brown sugar, oil, egg and buttermilk. Then stir in baking soda and vanilla. Lastly, mix in flour and apples. Pour batter into prepared pan. In a small bowl, combine sugar, cinnamon, and butter, mixing gently with a fork. Spread it evenly over the batter. It will not fully cover the batter, but it will bake up fine. Bake for 50-60 minutes or until golden brown. Serve warm or at room temperature.

Nutritional Values: Calories: 120 kcal / Carbohydrates: 45 g / Proteins: 12 g / Fiber: 7 g / Fats: 9 g

Fruit Cake

Total Time: 5 mins / **Prep. Time:** 5 mins /

Cooking Time: / **Difficulty:** Easy
Serving Size: 4 servings

Ingredients:
- 1 stick butter softened
- 1-pound all-purpose flour
- 1 cup pecans chopped
- 2 cups fruitcake fruit
- 2 cups sugar
- 2 eggs
- 1 tsp baking powder
- 1/2 tsp salt
- 1 tsp vanilla

Instructions:
You will use one 9×5" loaf pan for this. Spray inside with nonstick spray lightly and shake some flour in while patting it around so it slides out nicely when done. Preheat oven to 290 °F. In a bowl whisk sugar, eggs, vanilla together and then add softened butter and whisk until smooth. In another bowl whisk together dry ingredients. Then slowly incorporate this into your butter, wet, mixture. Gently fold in fruit and pecans so it is incorporated nicely. Then pour batter into your pan and bake for 1.5 hours until toothpick comes out clean. Cool in pan on wire rack for 9 minutes, then loosen slides with a knife and slide out. Set that on your cooling rack to completely cool. Slice and serve.

Nutritional Values: Calories: 80 kcal / Carbohydrates: 4 g / Proteins: 8 g / Fiber: 22 g / Fats: 2 g

CHAPTER 18: 30-Days Meal Plan

Day 1:
- Breakfast: Strawberry Smoothie
- Lunch: Grilled Chicken Salad
- Dinner: Baked Salmon with Quinoa
- Dessert: Kiwi Muffins

Day 2:
- Breakfast: Colorful Vegetables and Muesli
- Lunch: Zucchini Cheesy Lasagna Casserole
- Dinner: Teriyaki Sesame Beef Skewers
- Dessert: Mango Shake

Day 3:
- Breakfast: Caramelized Peach Quinoa Breakfast Bowl
- Lunch: Thai Cabbage Salad
- Dinner: Spicy Salsa Meatloaf
- Dessert: Chocolate Chip Cookies

Day 4:
- Breakfast: Simple Oat Waffles
- Lunch: Lentil Salad
- Dinner: Parmesan and Paprika Baked Cod
- Dessert: Strawberry Lemonade

Day 5:
- Breakfast: Protein Pancakes
- Lunch: Roasted Sweet Potato Taco Salad
- Dinner: Chicken Cacciatore
- Dessert: Microwave Chocolate Pudding

Day 6:
- Breakfast: Birchermuesli
- Lunch: Mediterranean Roasted Chickpeas
- Dinner: Garlic Alfredo Sauce over Spaghetti
- Dessert: Date Honey Nut Cake

Day 7:
- Breakfast: Banana Pancakes
- Lunch: Spinach & Tomato Frittata
- Dinner: Shrimp Alfredo Pasta
- Dessert: Summer Strawberry Shortcake

Day 8:
- Breakfast: Heart Healthy Overnight Oats
- Lunch: Mushroom Cauliflower Skillet
- Dinner: Beef Stew
- Dessert: Chocolate Black Bean Brownie Bites

Day 9:
- Breakfast: Baked Vegan Eggplant & Zucchini Chips
- Lunch: Chickpea Bean Curry
- Dinner: Skillet Shrimp Scampi
- Dessert: Kiwi Muffins

Day 10:
- Breakfast: Simple Egg Salad Sandwich
- Lunch: Roasted Brussels Sprouts
- Dinner: Chicken Quesadillas
- Dessert: Warm Apple Crisp

Day 11:
- Breakfast: French Apple Tarte
- Lunch: Balsamic Chicken
- Dinner: Teriyaki Sesame Beef Skewers
- Dessert: Whole Orange Almond Cake

Day 12:
- Breakfast: Baking Mix Soft Molasses Cookies
- Lunch: Coconut Curry Carrot and Sweet Potato Soup
- Dinner: Parmesan Chicken Cutlets
- Dessert: Chocolate Chip Cookies

Day 13:
- Breakfast: Pomegranate Banana Smoothie
- Lunch: Quinoa Salad
- Dinner: Trout with Garlic Lemon Butter Herb Sauce
- Dessert: Rainbow Fruit Salad

Day 14:
- Breakfast: Avocado Fries
- Lunch: Tomato, Beef, and Macaroni Soup
- Dinner: Blackened Salmon Tacos
- Dessert: Homemade Hot Chocolate Mix

Day 15:
- Breakfast: Healthy Pancakes
- Lunch: Cheesy Broccoli Rice Casserole
- Dinner: Ground Beef Tacos
- Dessert: Chocolate Black Bean Brownie Bites

Day 16:
- Breakfast: Carrot Oatmeal Greek Yogurt Muffins
- Lunch: Farmers Market Ramen
- Dinner: Spiced Beef Skewers
- Dessert: Kiwi Muffins

Day 17:
- Breakfast: Garlic Drop Biscuits
- Lunch: Basil Chicken in Coconut-Curry Sauce
- Dinner: Grilled Citrus Tilapia
- Dessert: Chocolate Chip Cookies

Day 18:
- Breakfast: Banana Oatmeal
- Lunch: Coconut Lentil Stew with Kale
- Dinner: Pulled Pork
- Dessert: Moist Pumpkin Cake

Day 19:
- Breakfast: Easy Pancakes
- Lunch: Spicy Southern Fried Catfish
- Dinner: Crock Pot Jamaican Jerk Chicken
- Dessert: Date Honey Nut Cake

Day 20:
- Breakfast: Baked Oatmeal Muffins
- Lunch: Grilled Asparagus
- Dinner: Garlic Alfredo Sauce
- Dessert: Lemonade

Day 21:
- Breakfast: Mediterranean Breakfast Sandwich
- Lunch: Roasted Carrots
- Dinner: Black Pepper Steak
- Dessert: Summer Strawberry Shortcake

Day 22:
- Breakfast: Spicy Beef Noodle Soup
- Lunch: Moroccan Rice Salad
- Dinner: Chicken Cacciatore
- Dessert: Chocolate Chip Cookies

Day 23:
- Breakfast: Peanut Butter Protein Overnight Oats
- Lunch: Lemon Chickpea Orzo Soup
- Dinner: Baked Beans from Scratch
- Dessert: Date Honey Nut Cake

Day 24:
- Breakfast: Baked Sweet Potato Fries
- Lunch: Healthy Choco Banana Cookies
- Dinner: Garlic Alfredo Sauce over Spaghetti
- Dessert: Rainbow Fruit Salad

Day 25:
- Breakfast: Simple Egg Salad Sandwich
- Lunch: Mediterranean Roasted Chickpeas
- Dinner: Heart Bolognese Sauce
- Dessert: Chocolate Black Bean Brownie Bites

Day 26:
- Breakfast: Heart Healthy Overnight Oats
- Lunch: Thai Cabbage Salad
- Dinner: Grilled Steak Salad
- Dessert: Kiwi Muffins

Day 27:
- Breakfast: Birchermuesli
- Lunch: Vegan Garbanzo Bean Curry
- Dinner: Creamy Tuna Salad
- Dessert: Whole Orange Almond Cake

Day 29:
- Breakfast: Zucchini Cheesy Lasagna Casserole
- Lunch: Roasted Brussels Sprouts
- Dinner: Blackened Salmon Tacos
- Dessert: Lemonade

Day 30:
- Breakfast: Homemade BBQ Sloppy Joes
- Lunch: Mushroom Cauliflower Skillet
- Dinner: Teriyaki Sesame Beef Skewers
- Dessert: Rainbow Fruit Salad

Day 28:
- Breakfast: Grilled Nectarine Salad
- Lunch: Coconut Curry Carrot and Sweet Potato S
- Dinner: Spicy Salsa Meatloaf
- Dessert: Chocolate Chip Cookies

Conclusion

Thanks for reading this book. Nutrition to keep your heart healthy is the basis of good health, excellent prevention of any ailment related to the heart (obviously), and the general maintenance of your best physical shape.

The bottom line, a heart-healthy diet is key to preventing heart problems. Some risk factors for heart problems include smoking, high blood pressure, and high cholesterol. Therefore, it's essential to be aware of these factors and do your best to manage them, such as by stopping smoking, keeping your blood at a healthy pressure, and maintaining a healthy cholesterol level. Symptoms of heart problems can include fatigue, shortness of breath, chest pain, and dizziness. In case of suspicious symptoms, it is essential to consult a doctor.

The American Heart Association's recommendations for preventing heart problems include getting regular physical activity and eating a healthy diet. A heart-healthy diet should consist of foods high in fiber, such as vegetables, fruits, legumes, and whole grains. These foods help lower cholesterol and keep the heart healthy. It's also important to limit your intake of saturated fat, sodium, and added sugars, which can increase your risk of heart problems. Drinking plenty of water and limiting alcohol consumption are other vital recommendations for keeping your heart healthy.

In summary, eating a heart-healthy diet and regular physical activity are essential for preventing heart problems. Awareness of the risk factors and symptoms of heart problems is equally important. Following these tips, you can take care of your heart and keep it healthy.

Equally important is keeping your body physically active and fit. In fact, the heart is a muscle that must be trained and kept busy over time.

A sedentary lifestyle and bad habits can seriously affect the overall health of your heart (and metabolism too). With the valuable information in this book, you will have an excellent tool to better manage the care of your heart and prevent future problems.

I jus t have to wish you a good life and a lot of joy.

Scan the two QR codes

Made in the USA
Las Vegas, NV
01 May 2024

89389834R00063